TRANSFORMATION SPRINT®

How to solve big transformation
problems in just 4 weeks

Fin Goulding   **Haydn Shaughnessy**

Praise for *Transformation Sprint*®

Haydn and Fin have got to the core of why transformations become too complex and run into difficulties that seem impossible to navigate for those trying to manage them. More importantly, they show how you can resolve those problems quickly. Pragmatic, practical and timely, they fill a gap in our knowledge of transformation, showing how to simplify the seemingly complex so that you can get back on a path to effective and sustainable transformation at pace.

TIM ELLIS, Founder and CEO, The Transformation People

The 'missing link'. Finally a book that effectively links the process of business model design/ redesign (the what and why) to the need for a dynamic engine of delivery, a generative operating model (the how) and goes on to provide a coherent blueprint and route map for achieving successful and sustainable, transformation, through transformation sprints (the how to). If you are involved in digital transformation, this book is essential reading.

ED CURLEY, Senior Programme and Project Manager, Digital Transformation

---

Transformation Sprint is essential reading for all transformation leaders. Too many digital transformations lose sight of what they're trying to achieve and run into problems. With *Transformation Sprint* Fin and Haydn provide a simple but powerful approach which in just 4 weeks opens the door to real change and avoids this trap - or just as importantly can get you out of the trap if you're already in it.

JOHN BOYES, Agile coach and CIO advisor

Most approaches to transformation will claim to be about improving business results but in reality they are IT centric. They may advocate setting business goals or OKRs but they jump right into changing the IT execution model, IT processes and tools and then expect the "magic" will happen. *Transformation Sprint* is fundamentally about improving your business operating model and not on a one time basis but giving you the mindset and tools to continually "remodel" it staying connected to your market as it changes and ahead of your competition. Haydn and Fin's approach is holistic and does include the IT side of the equation but you have to let your business operating model drive it. So whether you are just starting, in the middle of an existing transformation, or did not get the desired results from one you executed, *Transformation Sprint* will give you the structured approach, the tools and templates, the help you need to act fast with clear objectives and explicit deliverables that shows value in days not years.

CHARLES KENNEDY, Vice President, Huntington Bank

How can we overcome the structural challenges we face in business, economy and society, with COVID added on top? Organisations are scrambling to remodel themselves to be more relevant to customers' needs or more adaptive to the sheer scale of change. How do we ensure we can adapt? How do we start this remodelling and what levers should we apply? There are no simple answers to these questions nor are there likely ever be. But with *Transformation Sprint* you do get the means to uncover, communicate and act on the challenges - structurally and repeatedly. No enterprise architect's toolbox should be without it.

RON KERSIC Technology Strategy & Innovation, ING Bank

Leading a transformation means not to focus solely on tools, technology and products but also to take care of underlying structural, organizational and cultural challenges that could quickly turn into roadblocks. *Transformation Sprint* greatly supports leaders to get organized and start this journey.

JANKA KRINGS-KLEBE, Managing Partner co-shift GMBH and Chair, Digital Transformation committee of the Stuttgart Chamber of Industry and Commerce

---

Transformation Sprint is the best addition to a transformation professional's armoury since MSP was introduced in 1999. Its four main weapons are an insightful Generative Operating Model and the focused use of the Lighthouse Projects, the pace brought by an agile sprint approach, and finally an incredibly pragmatic delivery ethos. You get the picture. *Transformation Sprint* is instantly deployable, instantly relevant and instantly valuable. Its use will instil Board level confidence in transformation delivery.

CHRIS BARRETT, Co-Founder and CEO, Global Certification and Training Institute and Transformation Director

---

Organisational change is hard in its own right, only compounded by the fact that every organisation is unique and has a unique journey ahead of them. Yet across them all, there is a certain rhythm or cadence that underpins every journey. What Fin and Haydn have managed to do with *Transformation Sprint* is to highlight all the major touchpoints along this journey. There is something in this book for everyone, be they a business leader looking to understand the journey ahead of them, or a business consultant looking to see how best to help their clients.

EVAN LEYBOURN, CEO & Co-Founder, Business Agility Institute

As a senior exec in large organisations one of the hardest things to achieve is mobilising your team and your peers to focus on investment and deliver transformational change. This is a fantastic, expert guide for how to get your team to deliver a compelling vision, based on solid facts and with a clear, achievable plan. I wish I had this 20 years ago.

HUGH HESSING, Senior Executive,
Startup Advisor and Former COO of Aviva

Acknowledgements

We would like to acknowledge the many people who have helped us think through the method and description of Transformation Sprint.

For inspiration, we drew on the incredible body of work on Design Sprints at Google Ventures. The time-boxed efficiency of the design sprint helped us to shape our thinking on how to make transformation more effective.

We would like to thank Ron Kersic, future's architect, of ING bank whose busy schedule did not prevent him from adding wise advice from his extensive experience of transformation, to an earlier version of the book.

Tim Ellis at The Transformation People similarly read thoroughly and provided good advice. Evan Leybourn, founder of the Business Agility Institute, gave up his time to talk with us at various points and highlighted the need for practical information and guidance on full business transformation.

We have had regular conversations with Bart Weaver, senior agile coach at Nationwide Mutual Insurance, Columbus, Ohio, and Charles Kennedy, VP and Senior IT Service Delivery Manager, at Huntington Bank, on their approaches to transformation and this has allowed us to reflect a wider range of real life experiences. Presenting the wider Flow Framework at their 2019 Business Agility conference, in Columbus, Ohio, gave us a chance to talk with other professionals about our work.

Janka Krings-Klebe is a fellow practitioner whose endorsement of the method means a lot to us as does that of Ed Curley and John Boyes, two people whose day to day work involves facilitating big change. Inderjit Sandhu, Director at Agile Business Transformations Ltd, went to great lengths to give us line by line feedback, for which we are also very grateful.

Paidi O'Reilly, Jeremy Hayes and colleagues at the Digital Transformation Lab, Cork University Business School provided many informal conversations on transformation and, though our methods differ, it was valuable to us to see how others go about guiding and facilitating people in this difficult task.

Jon Jorgensen, Director of Agile Coaching at Project Brilliant, opened our eyes to other approaches too, while students at Trinity, Dublin and the attendees at our workshops at the Irish Computer Society, gave us an opportunity to test our ideas with people responsible for implementation. Daniel Vacanti provided us with insights on metrics and the low levels of productivity that follow in the wake of transformations and we would like to thank him for that insight and John Coleman, agile educator and trainer, for pointing out some of the strengths in Flow that even we weren't aware of.

We have also had many conversations with clients in Ireland, the US and UK, most of whom we can't name for confidentiality reasons. We owe them sincere thanks for trusting us to develop our methods as we worked with them.

Thanks finally to Eugenia Mantero, a highly respected agile practitioner who contributed advice and guidance based on her day to day real-world experience and expertise.

Benefits of this book

Most companies face structural or cultural problems and are trying to fix them with a transformation. Whichever type of transformation they choose (digital, agile, business etc.), they are on a journey from a current state, usually one where there is a good deal of dysfunction, to a new operating model, a future state, which they hope will be problem free.

It all sounds so simple, what could possibly go wrong? Well, more often than not they do. When that happens, a sense of helplessness can take over. How to fix major programs is a difficult enough question. But who should take responsibility? What will it cost? How can you design significant change programs so that they don't go wrong? How can we be sure they are holistic business transformations and not just something for IT, the usual focus of change?

These questions became suddenly more pressing once the COVID pandemic mutated in the collective consciousness from a short sharp disruption to an event that would change the way economies and society function. Now every company needs to transform but more so than ever. We can no longer afford the luxury of being tripped up by problems that are so commonplace that, in truth, they should have been dealt with years ago.

Despite the fact that problems are common, to date there has been no method to put matters right. But there is a relatively simple answer to the questions we posed above: *Transformation Sprint*, a time-boxed way to fix the big problems of transformation.

When transformation goes wrong, productivity can fall off a cliff (by one metric, according to expert Daniel

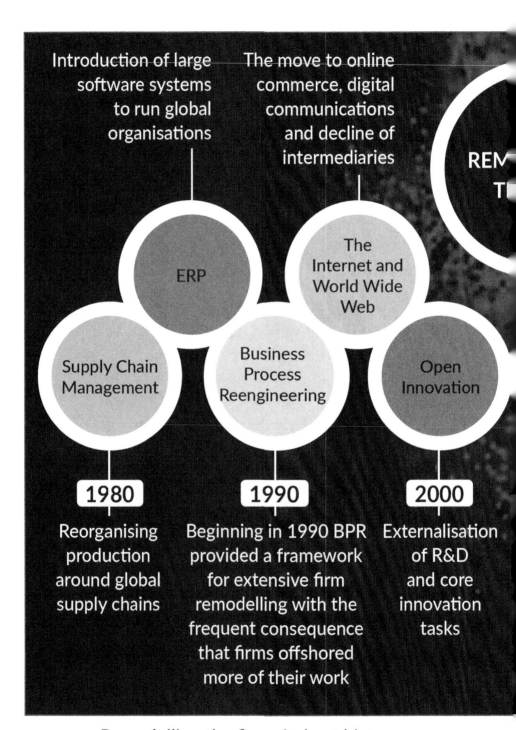

DIAGRAM 0.1 Remodelling the firm: A short history

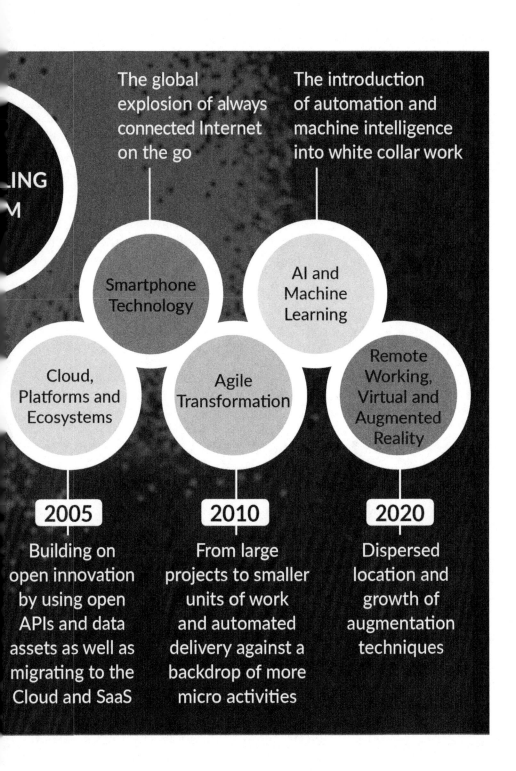

The global explosion of always connected Internet on the go

The introduction of automation and machine intelligence into white collar work

...ING
...M

Smartphone Technology

AI and Machine Learning

Cloud, Platforms and Ecosystems

Agile Transformation

Remote Working, Virtual and Augmented Reality

2005

2010

2020

Building on open innovation by using open APIs and data assets as well as migrating to the Cloud and SaaS

From large projects to smaller units of work and automated delivery against a backdrop of more micro activities

Dispersed location and growth of augmentation techniques

Vacanti, productivity can decline to around 10% of the norm). No problem, you might think, Transformations are a once in a generation activity. Not so!

When we set out to study the history of transformations, we found that businesses are faced with a transformation challenge roughly once every four years. As these overlap, a firm can be dealing with two or more journeys from their AS-IS to their desired target operating model, (by the way, we will use the acronym OM for operating model from time to time).

Looked at through that lens, most companies are always transforming something. They are perpetual remodelers. We have to think of transformation as a permanent state needing a well honed skill set.

Remodelling the business is not a taught skill at business school even though it is a constant pressure.

Added to that pressure is the fact that transformations require collaboration across different departments, supplier relationships and disciplines. For example, they need the cooperation of people in the business (product development, product marketing, innovation) with the IT department. Yet, there can be a long history of conflict and tension between these parties. IT can also be a source of dysfunction because of a long history of unresolved incompatibilities in technical platforms.

Very often, external consultants support transformation planning yet know nothing about the personalities involved and the histories of these conflicts and dysfunctions, nor of other significant impediments to change.

Most, if not all companies over twenty years old will be running different or incompatible IT systems that are difficult to wrangle into a new shape for the digital world.

Yet, the plan anticipates that all this dysfunction will just drop away.

So, you start your transformation against a backdrop of tension and potential conflict, with systems that don't align themselves well, advised by people with no great insight into your business, and then you layer in a whole new plan.

The odds of success are not in your favour. And it is no surprise when the finger-pointing starts.

We wrote Transformation Sprint to provide a method for getting these significant changes right. We also want to raise awareness of how underlying structural problems make transformations a supercharged emotional journey where people can quickly feel threatened.

By having Transformation Sprint to hand, we believe you can create a safer environment, better geared for success. You have a method to fall back on when tensions rise, and by taking time out for the Sprint, you can defuse conflict by giving everybody a standard practice, a common language and a shared purpose.

You will find this handbook and method invaluable, whether you are inside a company and responsible for change, or being invited in from the outside to help.

You could be an agile coach looking to advance her career or a project manager with responsibility for change programs. You might work in the digital transformation office, or you could be dealing with a problematic SAFe implementation. Maybe you are a CEO or a member of the leadership team looking for guidance on how to initiate and plan change or to save a program from difficulties. This book is for all of you.

The Transformation Sprint gives you a new way to approach big problem solving that is time-boxed, fast and effective. No waiting around while consultants get up to speed and expand their presence. No massive PowerPoint decks either.

These are practical steps you can take, either self-designing actual business transformations or fixing those that are going off course. It is also a prescription for how to become an agile business because agility is what you need if you are to serve customers better.

The methods take full account of the different perspectives that gather momentum and contribute to the challenges of change.

In transformations, all the emphasis is on the endgame for the company, the future state. The plan often overlooks the value of the systems and people that maintain the existing operating model. By giving equal weight to these, we hope you will avoid creating enemies within.

Our method will also deliver eye-opening insights into any dysfunction impeding your attempts to change. We show you how to identify the top 10 issues holding you back and a simple visual method for strong priority setting.

There is the keyword. Our methods are simple. They are also interactive and enjoyable ways to solve the big problems in a limited amount of time, providing techniques for coaches, managers and leaders to take control of difficult circumstances.

They feed directly into the new ways to work you are looking to build out, as well as improving your innovation capability.

Take a step with us into the post-COVID agile business, improving your own expertise and career prospects by making a big difference, in a short space of time.

CONTENTS

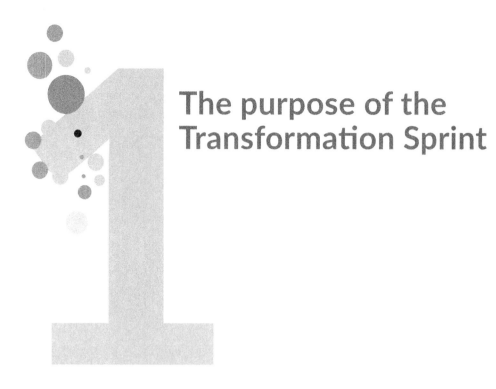

The purpose of the Transformation Sprint

In this chapter, we will provide the background business context for why transformation is currently so significant. We will also introduce the idea of the Transformation Sprint, and why we need speed and agility in transformations. We'll give you a working definition of the main terms.

The background

About twenty years ago, companies began to change the way they practised innovation and in the wake of that came a shakeup in corporate culture. The World Wide Web brought new champions to the fore in the shape of now familiar brands such as Google and Amazon. These companies were capable of continuously spinning up new ideas and new sources of value for customers. That in itself disrupted the competitive landscape. But it also introduced new and quicker ways to work, notably quicker ways to introduce new products, services and features.

The innovation industry went into overdrive with new incubators, accelerators, labs and ecosystems. All fixated on the idea of openness and the contribution of external parties to a company's future. But the emphasis also fell heavily on the notion of speed, and rapid iteration.

Meanwhile, the literature on innovation went on its own exponential growth curve. And the business model canvas and business model literature lay at the centre of it. A primary source of new value, people confidently asserted, was business model innovation.

What went unsaid and overlooked in the innovation dialogue is that many of the success stories from this era have involved changes to the operating model.

Most business model innovations require operating model innovations. Here's an example. The auto industry has increasingly relied on software services to increase customer satisfaction. Before introducing significant elements of software into the vehicle, the auto operating model revolved around the management of supply chains, the customised assembly of cars and the logistics (and relationships) of distribution. Those were the bare bones of their old operating model.

However, recently BMW announced that it needs to move to a new situation where half of its staff will be software developers. That change will help them to deliver the services that future travellers need (and to earn the revenue from them in new business models that embrace services).

The new business model is to tailor mobility services, probably in exchange for some kind of subscription or recurring revenue.

To support those services, it needs to remodel the company to incorporate 15,000 developers. The first, the switch in customer needs and revenues is the business model.

The second is the new operating model. The company will source those 15,000 developers from partnerships, recruiters, offshoring and so on. These activities and the rebalancing of labour types are a part of the operating model. The new partnerships that will deliver software, the sizeable contractual effort to secure their services, the code integration planning, and the cybersecurity needed, all represent the underlying services that enable the new mobility business model.

Think of the business model as a set of decisions about products and services relating to how a company earns revenue through customer relationships. The operating model comprises the services, systems, practices, platforms (and now more than ever the place of work and how to organise remote work) and the internal relationships that help deliver the business model.

In such transformations, executives and other leaders need to rethink what has become known as a target operating model, the endpoint of change.

And that's where many big names have fallen. In financial services alone, there have been fewer than a handful of companies that have managed to innovate both the business model and the operating model. Without the latter, you cannot do the former effectively. But while we have an abundance of business model literature, comparatively little is written about operating models.

In reality, though, companies are transforming their

operating models much of the time. They have changed how they function by introducing complex supply chains in the 1990s effectively giving production work away to third parties and instead becoming organisers and orchestrators. They have moved to offshoring, outsourcing, the introduction of robotics, switching from production lines to assembly lines and so on.

These changes take place frequently, and companies adapt on an ad hoc basis. There is a paradox in here waiting to be understood. Companies that struggle with transformation (the failure rate exceeds 80%) transform very often. There is another paradox too.

The literature on transformation and much of the consulting around it focuses on a fixed target operating model.

The evidence suggests we would be far better to think of generative operating models, i.e. operating models that continuously change. They would be stronger without a fixed destination.

Great companies create new operating models and remodel their businesses frequently. They achieve excellence in operating model design, but it is a generative process, a constant rethinking of what the model should be.

As a small example of that, the streaming video service Netflix decided at one stage on a radical HR plan. They would offer people money to leave. The offer was generous too. This bold new policy said to staff, we only want you if you are committed. That type of change is an operating model change because it adapts an essential process; in this case, employment incentives and engagement practices.

The operating model consists of the underlying systems and internal services, handovers, code and ways of work that allow you to seamlessly, and cost-efficiently spin up new business models.

It is the most crucial factor in adaptability or agility. Adaptability has become a skill of leaders at all levels in good companies. And just as important, it has to become a culturally accepted activity that does not trigger multiple immune system responses.

So how do you learn these skills?

In our COVID-damaged world, that is probably the most important question you can ask, as we seek ways to adapt whole economies to a new reality.

We are going to show you how to create the conditions for success in operating model design, which is another way of saying we have methods that will make transformations more likely to succeed.

Whether you are starting out on a transformation or taking responsibility for putting one right, you need to face the sad fact that most transformations are broken in some form or other. In the past, we have been able to absorb the cost of failure but in current circumstances it is critically important to have a stronger guarantee of success.

The existence of a broken transformation gives you an unparalleled opportunity to introduce methods that will make your operating model more generative and adaptable. You might even start to think of your objective as less of a target operating model and more of a generative one. That's where we want to get you to.

Our overall thinking on generative operating

models can be found at **The Transformation Sprint (thetransformationsprint.com)** website. In this book, we are going to focus on the start of that journey: Clarifying a target operating model, designing the right roadmap or fixing a transformation that has run into difficulties.

Having the skills to lead or participate constructively in a transformation is rare. Success comes from leaders and their previous experiences, of course. But it also depends on understanding how to design new operating models and identify the skills that will be needed when the transformation is in progress and when complete.

Some companies developed their operating model (OM) design skills early on. Amazon, for example, is an OM champion.

Their customer-centred innovations are often prosaic. They might spin out a new unit such as Amazon Business or Amazon Handmade. They have produced user-specific devices like Kindle. These are relatively standard innovations.

But on the other hand, what is truly remarkable about them is how they continue to design and build their organisation and infrastructure to deliver more value to customers, across more categories than any company ever has before (except for Alibaba).

This all began in the mid-2000s with a complete overhaul of the Amazon operating model, in particular its core platforms. The rationalisation of the core architecture is what allowed them to develop Amazon Web Services, which became one of the most successful companies in the world.

Over the past ten years, business excellence has become more and more dependent on executive teams, and the agilists who report into them, aiming for **operating model** *excellence* of this type. Good leaders should be able to manage operating model transformations with confidence.

Agile itself is part of a new operating model and it infuses many organisations. Agile frameworks such as SAFe have had notable successes in the extent of their implementations.

Nonetheless, the failure count is not coming down. Executives and team leaders do not yet know how to do transformation properly. The Transformation Sprint is an answer to that problem.

In this book, we are going to focus on how you can understand transformation in a new and different way. We are going to talk about how to fix them through a method that helps grow your transformation skills.

We are also going to look at how to begin the process of designing a new operating model. Whether your priority is Cloud, Digital, AI, Agile, RPA (Robotic Process Automation), the design principles are the same.

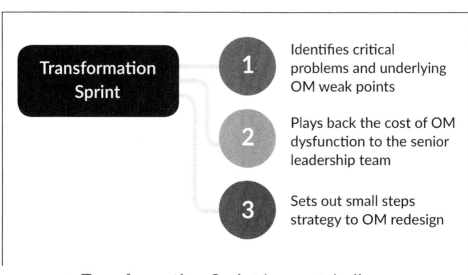

DIAGRAM 1.1. Transformation Sprint in a nutshell

We won't go any further than that. We are going to teach the skills to analyse the structural problems your company faces. You can solve the conflict and dissatisfaction around you by beginning the process of remodelling, simply and effectively.

In four weeks, you can set a transformation on the right course. Let's do it.

What is a Transformation Sprint? (the short version)

Has change ever seemed like a daunting challenge to you and your organisation? Do you bear the mental scars of conflicts that have brewed for years but break out across the firm when transformation activity stalls, dependencies get out of hand, deadlines slip, and you try one too many resets?

These are familiar experiences to many people, but the Transformation Sprint is your superhero, ACME strategy tool for engineering quick and valuable results.

But who are you? Chances are you are a communicator and a connector, a leader or coach whose role is to open people's eyes to new ways of working.

We don't expect you will be doing all the work we outline here. But you are an enabler and you can lead people on this incredibly fast journey to designing and unblocking stalled programs. Join us too on **The Transformation Sprint** website to connect with peers who are super-enablers just like you. There, we will be talking about how to design good transformations from scratch using the same methods.

Transformation Sprints:

- Draw on the agile principle of acting fast with clear objectives and explicit deliverables that show value in days not years.

- Provide a quick and thorough method for designing how to do good transformations or unblocking work in progress en route to a new operating model.

- Can be applied to an agile or digital change, enterprise transformation, the introduction of new work methods or getting the best out of the Cloud.

- Enable your and your teams to reach agreement on what needs to change and why.

- Support your quest to identify new and relevant capabilities for becoming a resilient, future-focused organisation.

- Help you grow business design (and redesign) skills, taking you closer to actual business agility.

They are also a great way to check in on a transformation and reset it before it goes wrong. We recommend mini-sprints as a six-monthly check-up. We'll go into more detail below, but here is the short and rapid definition.

The Transformation Sprint is a way to solve transformation problems, design transformations and build a better understanding of your future operating model—all within four (4) weeks.

Who needs a Transformation Sprint?

Leaders at all levels of a company need a common language and a simple technique for designing change. Transformations heighten emotions. They are daunting for people. They threaten to leave some behind while promoting others. They

can inspire people and raise the spirit of collaboration but they can also bring out primal fear. The result of that will often be the passive aggression that derails your best efforts.

You need techniques you can use to design the right transformation and to fall back on when the going gets tough. Method is essential for initial transformation design, for addressing blocked transformations, and for promoting the agile business.

The problem is you are probably starting your work with a raft of consultant reports and a model like Spotify or SAFe or a seven-point framework from a consulting firm.

Why is this a problem?

There are many reasons. One is that "the plan" tends to come in a vast swathe of PowerPoints that no team will be able to follow. The second is that the Spotify model is applied as if it is a transition to a fixed destination and unfortunately, set destinations are not helpful in transformations. And finally, frameworks like SAFe are logical but require a cultural uniformity that doesn't suit a single context. It can be a straightjacket that simply becomes another method that stalls progress.

You need something different: a design process or a fallback. Transformation Sprints are there for you.

Why sprints?

There's a good analogy between transformation sprints and marathon training. Of course, a transformation is a marathon, but most marathon runners train through sprints. They do their 20Kms, but they also do interval training, a series of sprints that build up anaerobic strength, a way of building endurance with reduced oxygen supply. Many companies jump straight into the marathon without including the sprints. When they hit a wall, they have no strength left to see the program through, and it descends into acrimony and conflict.

Just like we have skills and methods for designing products and services, we need skills and techniques for finding our way through the many tribulations of transformation. We need new skills for redesigning, or remodelling, parts of the business affected by:

- The need for increased innovation

- Disruptive market factors

- Becoming more responsive to competition and opportunity

- Having to migrate to new operating technologies such as Cloud, AI and ML, RPA and so on

That means plenty of people should share a common language and methods:

- CEOs and senior leaders

- The digital transformation office

- The PMO and project managers

- Team leaders

- Agile coaches

- Scrum Masters

- Intrapreneurs, fixers and enablers

Developing excellence in operating model design should be part of the transformation journey. It provides you with a way to link your need for continuous strategy improvement to the organisational capabilities that deliver strategic value.

Triggers for action

We recommend the Transformation Sprint takes place before significant transformation planning begins. In many cases, however, transformations are in mid-flight before their complexity begins to overwhelm leadership and teams.

Complexity routinely causes conflict because people become disoriented in situations where they can't see the big picture.

Transformations accentuate conflicts because many people see their roles change and maybe even become redundant. Very likely, the constant emphasis on legacy as a hindrance and the target operating model as good, will alienate the very people you rely on, the ones keeping the business infrastructure (platforms, IT services and so on) going.

Conflict gets worse over time because few people have the experience of leading others through significant change. When nothing is getting fixed, suspicion and mistrust grow.

If, on the other hand, there is a trigger reaction that says, let's launch a Transformation Sprint instead of beating each other up, it can be like calling a timeout. It is a valuable exercise in its own right. But it also provides people with space to rethink complexity.

In all cases, we prefer simplification to the alternative of trying to live with and wrangle complexity. We believe that complexity is a sign of bad design or design gone wrong. Simplification should be your goal, though unfortunately there is a strong tendency to create big, complex projects.

Against that background, the trigger for the Transformation Sprint can be one or more of the following:

- An awareness that several aspects of a transformation are not meeting expectations.

- The arrival of new senior people (CEO, CIO, COO, CMO) who have a well-worked out change agenda.

- An awareness that major innovations impact the company at the system level, for example, becoming more data-centric or adopting AI.

- Engagement with a major consultancy is disappointing.

- Acknowledgement that silos of activity are harming the company.

- The desire for a more collaborative culture inside the organisation.

- The need to hire more exciting talent and develop new skills.

What is a Transformation Sprint? (long version)

The Transformation Sprint is 4 weeks long. Its focus is:

1 Identifying and analysing the problems that a dysfunctional operating model (OM) causes in a business transformation.

2 Logging the top ten issues for action.

3 Providing a solution, or solutions, to the underlying structural problems causing the dysfunction.

4 Creating a draft of a future, or target, operating model driven by those solutions.

5 Helping to design a better way of creating value and

testing new ways to work by identifying a suitable Lighthouse Project that will give you the learning and skills to transform in a better, more generative way.

Some term definitions before we go any further:

An operating model. Think of it as the constellation of technical infrastructure and services or core platforms (IT/ML); functional services (finance, HR, logistics etc.); capabilities - cybersecurity capability, innovation and value discovery capability, value management and delivery, etc.; and the firm's internal and external ecosystems.

A _Lighthouse Project_ is a term we use to describe the project that can help grow new capabilities in these areas, particularly in remodelling the business.

In transformations, a frequent problem lies in the sheer scale of change companies try to make. Apart from change being difficult in its own right, companies do not anticipate the new skills and work interactions they will need in their future operating model. In effect, they are creating a working model that they do not have the skills to manage.

One of the techniques we are going to explain is how to scale a transformation back to one critical, short term project that can provide useful lessons about the skills needed to manage structural change.

That initial project is the Lighthouse Project. It is not a prototype nor a Minimum Viable Product (MVP). The purpose is to identify the most critical, initial structural changes to make, along with the skills needed and the new ways of work that will deliver change over time!

Lighthouse projects are those initiatives that great companies use to arrive at a better structural model and more constructive ways to work.

The Lighthouse Project needs to address those structural changes by embracing new ways to work, and it also needs to demonstrate that the Lighthouse team can create value in a sprint, i.e. in the short term. The outline of a Lighthouse Project is the end goal of your Sprint. A transformation could have multiple Lighthouse projects because there are often several blockers, but for the sake of simplicity in this book, we assume one Transformation Sprint = one Lighthouse Project.

In summary, a Transformation Sprint should:

- Be capable of solving a structural problem in the OM through a Lighthouse Project

- Prove itself as a mechanism for creating new value

- Embrace new ways to work

Transformation Sprints and agile businesses

The Transformation Sprint distills complex information about the state of the firm, its future operating model and the route to change. Although it deals in abundant information, done right, the Sprint gives you a fast-track to total business agility. Few companies progress this far, or have done to date.

Often when companies start with transformations, their first step is to focus on agile software delivery. The IT department goes agile, and the rest of the business is barely affected. The diagram opposite shows the types of activities covered in what typically would be called an agile transformation.

DIAGRAM 1.2. Agile activity in a firm

VALUE DELIVERY

Agile Methods (Scrum etc)

DevOps

Continuous Delivery

Cloud

Test & Learn

IT AGILE

In a Transformation Sprint, we generally assume these activities are underway. Problems usually emerge not so much in these activities but in the interaction (or handover of work) between different parts of the business.

Once the business has gone IT agile, there are high expectations for broader increases in innovation. However, that relies on other departments embracing some kind of agile philosophy.

In practice, many transformation plans fail to take into account the full spectrum of business needs. A disconnect exists between agile delivery and the process of redesigning the enterprise so that it can succeed in changing markets.

The following diagram illustrates agile methods that take a business closer to full agility.

DIAGRAM 1.3. Frequently missing pieces of agile transformations

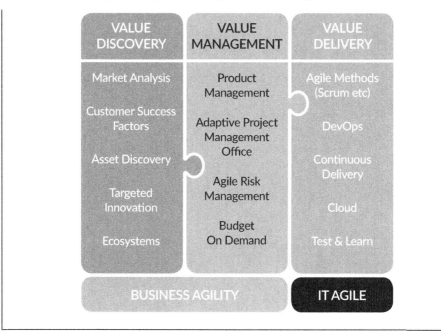

It is crucial to move left from value delivery to better value management and value discovery (a broader concept than innovation) to become "business agile".

Taking the far left column first, companies do practice different innovation methods these days. These are lean rather than agile and tend to add to the IT backlog of work in a way that outstrips resources. Flow value discovery tools help with this (you can consult them on *The Transformation Sprint* website).

In value management, there may be an adaptive portfolio philosophy, but other practices can confuse. For example, a product manager in the scrum team in IT and also in marketing, have ill-defined roles in relation to each other. And there is often no agile risk management nor agile budgeting

The diagram opposite represents a perfect outcome. In reality, these changes create a problematic scenario with overburdened teams, too much context switching, conflict, passive aggression and other adverse work conditions.

Management teams often react to this negativity as if they are being challenged, impeded or ignored. They feel their authority is threatened. What they don't take account of is the way that change management creates adverse conditions, which typically provoke emotional conflicts that surface during the Sprint's Perspective Gathering exercise. The Transformation Sprint is an excellent way to take a timeout to deal with them.

If you look at the final diagram, you will see where the tools of the Transformation Sprint fit. They take you beyond business agility to a new level of capability. But

DIAGRAM 1.4. The journey of an agile business

TRANSFORMATION SPRINT	VALUE DISCOVERY	VALUE MANAGEMENT	VALUE DELIVERY
Perspective, Analysis, Issues	Market Analysis	Product Management	Agile Methods (Scrum etc)
AS-IS State and Definition of TO-BE Future Business	Customer Success Factors	Adaptive Project Management Office	DevOps
	Asset Discovery		Continuous Delivery
Leadership Playback	Targeted Innovation	Agile Risk Management	Cloud
Definition of a Lighthouse Project	Ecosystems	Budget On Demand	Test & Learn

THE AGILE BUSINESS

they do imply that your long term goal is to get better at value management and value discovery too. The Transformation Sprint framework can help with that.

It takes time and dedication to become good at operating model design, but Transformation Sprints are a way to start. They offer a framework for figuring out what is wrong and how to put it right.

Most importantly, they allow you to scale the challenge back to something manageable. That also helps create a learning environment for remodelling and new ways to work, which you can then scale back up.

The role of mini-sprints

The sprint concept can and should apply to various aspects of the transformation process.

Transformations run into trouble in predictable areas. They break down when there's a transition to faster innovation or when introducing new platforms to service new products. These are often the main focus of Transformation Sprints - i.e. to fix or reset them.

However, the techniques operate equally well in any area of a firm that needs to transform. For instance, HR needs to become more agile, in line with a younger workforce, anticipating future skills' needs. Finance needs to simplify age-old accounting systems or switch to subscription or other recurring revenue models. Security needs to implement Cyber agility techniques, etc..

Sprints are a way to break down these challenges and move the whole body of transformation work on. Examples of where sprints can be applied are also on **The Transformation Sprint** website but here are a few to think about:

1 *Value discovery: Innovation process redesign*, through value discovery, creating far more efficient ways to innovate and aligning innovation work more precisely with market needs This too takes only one week, but it ensures your transformation is aiming at the right economic outcomes.

2 *Value Management: Portfolio rationalisation*, checking which projects align with corporate goals. This can be one of the biggest money savers and create a far more engaged workforce but takes only three weeks.

3 *Value delivery: Dependency management and improved workflow design*, a one week sprint will deal with dependency problems that can suck up a vast amount of resources.

4 *Value streams: Increasing the relevance of customer journey mapping*, an overlooked skill at least in terms of the whole journey a customer takes. Taking one team and nailing online-to-offline customer journey mapping would benefit most transformations.

5 *Value management, for project managers.* Most projects are designed as sequential activities rather than value-based activities. Very often, project overruns occur because of the design principles and how these relate to the overall dependency matrix in the company. Value-based project management means breaking work down by asking the question: what can I do next that has value, rather than asking: what is the typical sequence of work.

6 *Learning mechanisms, HR future-proofing.* HR needs to contribute more to the future body of required skills, and a two-week sprint can go a long way defining these.

All the evidence suggests that transformations regularly

hit the rocks. A substantial percentage fail to meet expectations. And often the disappointment runs over a period of years. On top of that, operating models should change regularly so even if you have designed the right transformation, you will want to keep returning the model.

Mini-sprints are a pared-back version of the Transformation Sprint. They give you a two week run at resetting your transformation goals and key Lighthouse Projects or taking stock of your current thinking about the new OM. We will emphasise throughout the book that you need a generative operating model or remodelling skills. Mini-sprints are a way to keep you re-tuning your sense of what kind of OM you need.

In the mini-sprint, you retain the perspective gathering, issues document, AS-IS state and target operating model analysis, Playback and Lighthouse Design. You can afford to forego the document research analysis. At the same time, however, you need to focus the perspective gathering on the short term experience of the actual transformation itself. What is working and what's not.

The phases of the Sprint

The Transformation Sprint takes place in six main Phases. We'll spell them out below. The Phases overlap so while you work on Phase 1, you will also be working on Phase 2 and Phase 3.

There are some prerequisites to making the sprint work well.

Before you start, secure

- Access to senior executives, as interviewees and as the decision-making body

- Good interaction with a sponsor inside the firm who has the trust of senior executives

- An administrator who will set up interviews and make sure other people's diaries align with the project

- Preferably dedicated office space

Given those prerequisites, here are the Phases.

TABLE 1.1. The phases of a Transformation Sprint

1	Perspective Gathering	Interviews to uncover different perspectives on the problems (Day 1 onwards)
2	Analysis	Market analysis and technical literature analysis (Day 4 onwards)
3	Issues Document	Logging the major issues (Day 1 onwards)
4	Describing the AS-IS and Future Operating Model	In draft form (Day 12 onwards)
5	Playback	To the executives and with prioritisation as a target (day 13 or 15)
6	Lighthouse Outline Design	Days (16 -20)

PHASE 1: Perspective gathering from DAY 1 onwards. We use about ten days on interviews, though patterns emerge early on, which you can record in a draft Issues Document.

PHASE 2: Concurrent with Phase 1, we access and begin analysing a range of business strategy and technical documents. We will show you later a set of templates for doing this and more are available on our website.

PHASE 3: The Issues Document. We build a list of significant issues from the interviews and the documentation. The list will start long but eventually, reduce down to 10.

PHASE 4: Describing the company's AS-IS state and a draft of any emerging target operating model(s). This usually involves describing dysfunctionality in the firm, often caused by incomplete transformations and the coexistence of two or more competing operating models.

PHASE 5: Playback. A day-long or at least half day playback with senior leaders where they prioritise issues and make real decisions.

PHASE 6: The outline design of a Lighthouse Project that will address dysfunctionality and set the transformation up for success as well as bring you critical experience in thinking in new ways about target operating model design.

That's the brief version but consult any of the chapters for more detail.

The importance of the operating model

In this chapter, we are going to discuss operating models. The reason for the deep dive is that there is no real tradition of operating model design inside many companies. Put that another way. They do redesign and remodelling in response to specific opportunities, say, for example, crypto-currencies for a bank.

But often they run into trouble because they have not been adequately equipped to do this thinking. It is not explicitly on their agenda as a skill set.

Executives know they need this skill, and the Transformation Sprint can help grow it. Nonetheless, it is a problematic area because of a lack of research and education.

The business context

Changes in the broader economy are forcing executives to review their company operating models (OM). It is fair to say that the OM is a new focus of innovation.

In recent years we have seen startups and born-digital companies create novel business models where there is a very low level of physical asset investment and no traditional value chain.

Examples include some of the best-known companies such as Airbnb and Uber. But even large, established companies, including Mercedes and BMW, have gone down this route, in particular, to replace revenues made from cars with revenues from services.

We have also seen a far higher degree of service integration from Chinese companies. Their services typically integrate e-commerce, logistics, finance and various types of goods and digital services (such as insurance). Alibaba is the prime example.

Even a company like Spotify is, in reality, highly integrated. We know it as a streaming music service. Bands allow Spotify to stream their albums and tracks to listeners in return for a small fee. But Spotify's business also supports musicians to record their music and to build their brand; it allows listeners to purchase tickets to events, so it also has to ingest content on band touring activities. It also has a very active editing team creating playlists. It has several joint ventures including one that looks after enterprise streaming (for example allowing retail outlets to use playlists that customers can influence). Companies are trying to deliver to the full range of a customer's needs.

Another change is the sheer scale of activity some companies now engage in. Alibaba can efficiently deliver over 350,000 sales per second at peak throughput.

We are probably also all now quite familiar with platform and ecosystem models that bring people together around a marketplace. We're less familiar with businesses that take a pure ecosystem approach, yet the workings of Amazon books platform is highly dependent on an ecosystem that Amazon does not own.

We are all in the habit of thinking about these as business model changes. But how true is this?

Is a marketplace a business model innovation? Humanity has been operating markets for millennia.

What is changing is the underlying operating model (OM) that allows companies to match parties to a market or to process millions of orders per second.

Many companies struggle with these new ideas and new capabilities because their underlying structures are already broken.

They begin transformation at a disadvantage. There is very little literature on how to do the nuts and bolts of change.

As an example, OM design requires managers to dig into their portfolios and decide which business lines to retire so that they can simplify their systems and infrastructure.

That might sound like an odd claim. Why can't business just keep on doing the same old things and add a bit on? The answer is because they maintain highly complex internal technology stacks that don't work very well. And are often made up of code that few people now understand.

To retire this legacy, they must retire lines of business or find something more attractive to offer to the customers that are currently supported by legacy.

The literature on retiring business lines and retiring legacy systems, however, is paltry compared to the research on innovation. The literature on how to remodel

operations, services and practices in response to innovation is equally small. Nonetheless, real innovation cannot happen unless firms address these issues.

But these are just two of the nuts and bolts of change. The consequence of not understanding these details of OM design is that transformations run into trouble. Transformation Sprints are an answer to these challenges. Transformation Sprints:

- Create a skill set in operating model design and innovation.
- Help rescue a failing transformation.
- Align operating models with innovation programs.
- Avoid investment in large transformation programs until enough is known about appropriate TOM design and the skills needed to deliver it.
- Help a company take the right steps to a more sophisticated OM as they change.

These are all facets of operating model design or what we call remodelling. Because the majority of such projects fail to meet expectations, we created the Transformation Sprint, the quickest and most reliable way to achieve operating model design excellence.

What is the operating model?

An operating model includes all the systems, capabilities, processes, services, ways of working (or practices) and even the locations that support a company in discovering value, managing value and delivering value.

Operating model redesign lies behind all types of company transformations. Logically, you transform from one operating model to a new one. Yet the topic of operating model redesign has been pretty much off-topic.

One challenge is the deep fear that any change to "how we get things done" will destabilise business execution.

In place of OM design, companies are offered a model or framework such as the Spotify model or SAFe, a value stream framework. The main difference in these frameworks is that they are generally non-contextual. They impose work practices and rules rather than opening up the opportunity to look at your specific context. We believe that context discovery is key to good transformation design.

Companies have access to some concepts around this issue, to help them decide, but not many. They talk about an AS-IS state; in other words, a description of how they currently add-value and get things done. They have aspirations to move to what might be called a TO-BE state, or a future operating model, a Target Operating Model (or TOM).

They also talk about the need for a business architecture. But the language and analytical tools stop just about there.

Paradoxically, businesses have been remodelling for years without actually thinking too deeply about it.

We will look at patterns of transformation later, but in our estimation, companies transform once every four or five years. They are always managing at least two transformations at once (introducing robotics, extending supply chains, offshoring, moving online and so on).

Right now that could be an agile transformation (ways of work), digital transformation (transforming systems and ways of work), the introduction of AI and machine learning (for example robotic process automation) and the development of business ecosystems.

It is surprising that this topic is under-developed but that leads people, at the planning stage, to overlook or gloss over challenges that will derail the transformation later.

Companies that we interact with are typically operating with a core technology stack that suffers from fundamental incompatibilities, not just within the stack itself but also between what the technology is capable of and what the company needs if it is to offer the market new value propositions at pace.

These situations infuse companies with gross inefficiencies that get hidden away because business leaders don't understand them and because it is easier to save costs by firing people rather than solving structural problems.

Many of the business people we meet do not understand what their technology can offer. They have their own aspirational language around a single view of the customer, for example, not realising that the project to create that could take four years. In the meantime, they overlook more straightforward ways to generate customer insight.

We also see cybersecurity continuing to look like an accident waiting to happen rather than a source of differentiation and value.

A way to solve these types of problems would be to bring business and IT together to review the structural problems that are holding a transformation back and the road out of them. That's what a Transformation Sprint does. That's first base though. In the longer-term companies need to commit to a generative operating model.

A generative operating model is one where people have the skills to generate new designs for "how things get done". Adopting a generative operating model and learning OM remodelling skills should be treated with some urgency, especially in the post-COVID era. We see too many instances when getting rid of FTEs (full-time equivalents) takes the place of well-constructed remodelling exercises that will remove significant waste (in place of firing talent).

Those remodelling skills would include not just analysing and describing how companies should change their processes but also what that means for how people work, how they interact and the many new skills they need.

The reality is that we are frequent remodelers of value-adding activity because getting it right creates a competitive advantage.

Go back to early factory models, and the company tended to buy in raw materials and then do all that was needed to make these into products. It would then ship those products out via wholesalers (or distributors).

That OM could be called an internal OM. From early on, though, the internal OM began to incorporate external partners.

For example, in the auto industry, early operating models were production and assembly-based (Ford would have a casting shop where it made its own engines ready for insertion on the assembly line). But already a key component (tyres) was being supplied by external companies (such as Goodyear).

Over time auto-makers realised that having specialised suppliers for components such as brakes, and later for telemetry and mapping, provided them with more space to concentrate on their core business. Over even more time, that core became less about producing the car, and more about servicing the car with components and after-sales.

The switch to a business model based on accruing profit from after-sales, came with numerous shifts in operating models to hone the car maker's craft in running dealerships and coordinating supplies.

The OM shifts were things like:

- developing a tiered supply chain model with Tier 1 suppliers working closely on future car capabilities.

- Tier ones managing Tier 2 suppliers.

- The introduction of enterprise resource planning (ERP) systems that could monitor global supply chains.

- And the development and professionalisation of the buying function.

- The development of inventory and ordering systems for globally distributed dealerships.

- Large IT departments to develop applications for procurement, component ingest, dispatch, and so on.

Since the mid-1990s, much of the emphasis in target operating model design has been on embracing the power of digital communications. This has allowed pioneering companies to take control of large segments of economic activity:

- Apple and Google and mobile Apps.
- Spotify and global music production and distribution.
- Google and Here with global mapping.
- Amazon and Alibaba and global e-commerce.
- Netflix and YouTube and global video streaming.

These companies have been good at rationalising their internal systems (what we call their core platforms) and developing the new skills needed to deliver products and services in new ways. They can create processes or human-machine architectures that make the management of large amounts of activity possible rather than dauntingly complicated.

We believe the ideal operating model to be a set of such practices (in addition to the processes, capabilities, systems, location of work, new ways of work and services that we have mentioned above).

That set of practices has to take account of the emotional burden of change and identify where conflict arises. Transformations can be full of friction caused by fundamental structural problems. Operating models need practices that address those types of issues, as well as straightforward technical change.

The diagram opposite shows the areas of practice we think are most important. We've ordered them into a generative framework. In this book, we are describing those two bookends at the left and right of the diagram.

DIAGRAM 2.1. The elements of a generative operating model

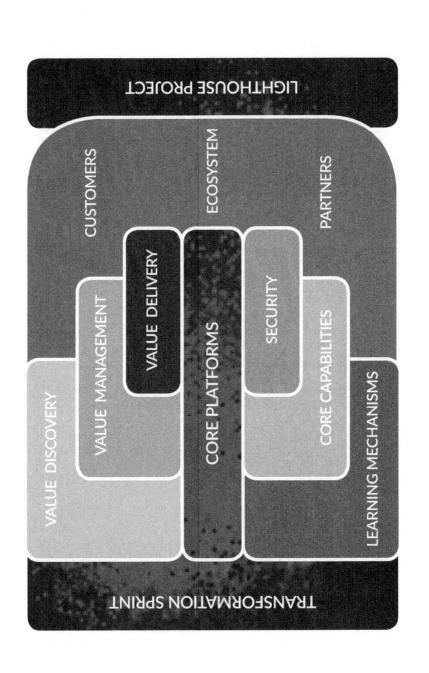

LIGHTHOUSE PROJECT

CUSTOMERS

ECOSYSTEM

PARTNERS

VALUE DISCOVERY

VALUE MANAGEMENT

VALUE DELIVERY

CORE PLATFORMS

SECURITY

CORE CAPABILITIES

LEARNING MECHANISMS

TRANSFORMATION SPRINT

A better definition of an operating model would embrace the idea of "practices and remodelling". The generative operating model is:

A set of practices designed to support the modelling and remodelling of the processes that allow us to discover, manage and deliver value to customers, at a profit.

Transformation Sprints and the operating model journey

Our objective in the first phase of a Transformation Sprint is to help the company to understand and visualise its transformation challenges. Typically, at some stage, this will involve the operating model.

When a transformation has become problematic, leadership teams can feel overwhelmed by the complexity it brings and loses sight of where they have to get to, assuming it was evident in the first place.

DIAGRAM 2.2. Transforming from AS-IS to TO-BE (Target Operating Model)

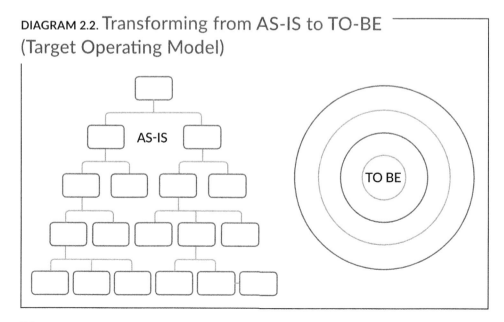

They will be transitioning from a problematic AS-IS state to a target operating model that might be well documented by consultants. Still, it may not be appropriate to their context (another failure point).

The emergent target operating model (TOM) might be any of these in the table below. In the table, we have given the model type in the left column a brief description in the middle column and issues arising in the right-hand column.

This table can act as an aide-memoire when you come to assess TOM states. In general, we find that there are usually two conditions on the ground.

In condition 1, the firm will have taken on a distinct model (Spotify, SAFe) and there will be a substantial personal investment on the part of some executives committed to the model rather than the outcomes.

In condition 2, a new model is emerging but is indistinct. This happens when companies aim for a digital or agile transformation. In fact what happens is they naturally gravitate towards data-centric models or platform models, for example.

You can spot those emergent target operating models in the Transformation Sprint and help outline a plan to draw them out more clearly.

TABLE 2.1. Types of target operating models and their challenges

1 **The Spotify Model**	Focused around new team arrangements
2 **The ING Model**	Platform and ecosystem-based with a high degree of customer enablement
3 **Agile / SAFe**	The predominant framework for scaling scrum teams and value stream management
4 **Digital / Business Agile**	Shifting out of physical processes (bricks and mortar, paper based record keeping) to digital
5 **Data centric**	Driven by the belief that data about customers and markets provides a decisive competitive advantage.
6 **Integrated**	Attempting to provide a full set of services to customers In the way Alibaba does
7 **Asset Lite**	Attempts to add content or data services to existing assets.

It can confuse because it is centred on new labels for teams that are not always reflected in substance but becomes a new set of rules.

It does not replicate the features of a platform and ecosystem business and is driven more by a concern to enable customers. After five years, ING believes its main gain has been recognition of autonomy to deliver enablement among the workforce.

Tends to create confusion over scaling agile teams as a goal in itself within a large framework that brings new disciplines. A tendency for people to feel lost in the new rules. Does not address core platform issues.

Very vendor-driven, with multiple new platforms available, including pure Cloud or SaaS services. Often compromised by the lack of coherence in core platforms and insufficient planning to retire old business lines.

Tends to stall on major data clean up and management issues (master data management).

Takes exceptional talent and clean IT slate.

Philips in lighting, Prepd (lunchboxes, cookware and apps) in the startup community are trying to do this and to date, we have not experienced any serious issues arising.

Getting ready for the sprint

Being in good shape for a sprint is imperative, so what does it take?

In this chapter, we will cover:

- Who should do the work
- Working either as an internal or external change agent
- How to set the right expectations
- The kind of team you need to assemble to execute the sprint well
- Recognition of the emotional journey
- The tools you need, some of which we provide in this book
- Some prerequisites
- The possibility of future mini-sprints to keep teams on course

Who should do the work

Transformation Sprints can be run by anybody competent in winning trust and analysing problems. Your background could be in agile coaching, design thinking, business analysis, process management, project management or IT. You could be a leader at any level of the organisation.

The techniques we recommend require no esoteric skills, other than somebody on the team needs to understand IT and somebody else needs to understand business strategy.

The general skills are: being able to put people at ease, listening to what people have to say, winning the ear of a strong sponsor, and then being able to follow the Transformation Sprint method or having the ability to adapt it to your own specific context.

Much of the analytical work you will do can draw on our templates for business analysis and IT analysis. You will find them on our website.

It might be that you engage with an external consultant, skilled in Transformation Sprint methods. Or a consultant you trust to run the sprint, based on those methods. There is no significant learning curve in the technique itself. We have set that out in an orderly way so you can concentrate on the problems in front of you.

The Transformation Sprint is a framework for developing significant insights that will help you unlock broken transformations or help you design a good one from the start. But the method does not require specialist skills beyond empathy and analysis.

Working as an internal change agent or external consultant

You will be working under different constraints depending on whether you are an internal or external change agent. As external practitioners, we find companies call us in when transformation problems have begun to reach the unmanageable stage. At least one person in senior management will recognise that they have run out of internal solutions.

Given that we offer this short and insightful exercise, we don't find massive resistance to the prerequisites we outline. These are mostly concerned with executive time allocation, access to whomever we want to interview and the free availability of critical documents.

In return, we are offering a time-boxed process. Both of those are important. It is a process, so it is manageable merely by asking what stage you are at? And it is time-boxed, so it is not going to grow or expand and become a financial liability. The project is so small that we don't find it necessary to offer measurable outcomes or to include metrics in our proposal.

We promise the outline of a Lighthouse project that will scale their problems back to a manageable degree and provide a way forward.

What we do as well is offer alternatives. We are happy to start by reviewing the portfolio of work or by looking at the firm's innovation processes. Generally speaking, these alternatives have proven less attractive than the Transformation Sprint because the sprint is so time-boxed.

Working as an internal agent will be different. The major constraint will be around company objectives. Without

wishing to insult anybody, we often find that companies do not have a clear vision, mission or goals; and even when they do have these, much of the investment they are making does not ladder up to them. They commission projects that last too long and will never meet a goal and they commission initiatives that don't relate to their goals.

The constraint for an internal change agent is that these inconsistencies do need to be addressed. Both you and your sponsor will be asked to delineate an outcome that helps meet specific objectives, but you will be aware that there is much inconsistency around goals.

Our advice on this is to play down the broader implications of the sprint. In other words, create space to do something short and to the point to see what comes of it. Resist the existing metrics suite if at all possible. We also find resistance to the idea of a "reset" in transformations. Senior leaders don't like the idea that their program needs to be reset or re-baselined. Sell it instead as a health check or a time-out and as a way of introducing agile methods into transformation governance, i.e. using the agile sprint to manage the transformation is evidence of changing the way of working.

Setting expectations

There are times when it pays to aim low and set modest expectations but this is not one of them. The promise is "significant progress in four weeks."

Because you are promising momentum, people must realise they have to invest small amounts of their time. This has implications for everybody involved. For example, it raises the imperative that senior leaders will make themselves available in a given timeframe or fall out of the loop.

You also need to commit to identifying the top 10 issues blocking change and help to prioritise these before you go on to solution design. And you will do this in a short timeframe.

Here's a short list of expectations you can set.

1 *The need for senior leadership time and access*. One of the first things to do is to set an agenda around the moments when you will need access. That is especially the case for Playback and the final outline Lighthouse Design presentation. But you also need 30 - 60 minutes of each leader's time for one-to-one interviews.

2 *Identifying the top 10 blockers and issues.* There is no room, and no reason, for slippage on this one. You promise the top 10 and need to explain their significance.

3 *Prioritisation.* Prioritisation is a critical element of Playback, so more on this later. But promise prioritisation as most leadership teams fail to prioritise. You are doing them a big favour.

4 *Do not promise a full transformation design.* You need to be clear you are giving a solution to the most pressing problems. You are going to set up new ways to work and to solve a structural problem in a transformation. However, you are not designing the transformation or the Lighthouse Project (that's for the Lighthouse team to do). You can give the outline, the rationale and objectives.

5 *Do emphasise momentum.* Everybody will expect the time to slip. Be on top of this from the word go. Make sure you have the Playback pencilled in for week three and the final report for Day 20. Get senior time commitments to these dates.

What kind of team do you need for a Transformation Sprint?

We believe in keeping teams small and generally for a Transformation Sprint that means a maximum five people. Here are their roles:

1 *Enabler:* perhaps an agile coach or similar who is fully committed to making the sprint happen, keeping it on track and building momentum but as important, able to build empathy with and support from everybody the sprint touches.

2 *IT expert:* a person whose expertise stretches across IT functions and has experience of leadership interaction at a high level, unfazed when the pressure builds, or executive participants at the Playback become defensive. High credibility yet able to talk with developers, coaches, and doers across the business.

3 *Analyst:* we want to say super-analyst, a person who can quickly get to the bottom of things, with an ability to assimilate information. Templates and checklists should support that skill so he/she can move to conclusions fast. Should be able to build templates based on experience across different companies or adapt ours (see **The Transformation Sprint** website) on topics like common structural problems and issues, business strategy weaknesses, competitive conditions.

4 *Business or tech sponsor:* from the executive team, the person who believes in change and can commit to speed, has enough contacts to make sure the perspective gathering draws on the right interviewees.

5 *Graphics' support:* a graphics or design expert who knows how to build visual stories and is light on personal

maintenance, i.e. won't get upset when you tear the graphics down and get a second iteration underway.

Recognition of the emotional journey

We said earlier that transformations have a habit of raising the emotional temperature. There are several reasons for this, and you should make yourself aware of all of them. Also, explore your own context for how and why people become defensive.

1 *Treating staff as legacy:* Companies have legacy technology problems that are often part of the transformation objective, i.e. reduce legacy. The people who manage legacy technology read that as "get rid of people like me". They endure months, if not years, of uncertainty and they derail programs if they are not treated with respect. You have to be on the lookout for this. You cannot solve it, but you can flag it as a severe progress blocker and propose ways to improve the situation.

2 *The IT-Business divide:* Just as common as the legacy person, there is a simmering conflict between IT and the business. Cooperation between the two is essential to the transformation. However, business will be complaining that IT is not cooperating and IT will complain that business people do not understand their constraints. This conflict bubbles up in transformations. We have found that most IT shops are overworked for the wrong reasons, and most business people fail to understand their business environment. That's not to say both sides are wrong or right, but sensitivity to how this conflict plays out in front of you in interviews and structural problems is critical.

3 *The legacy of past lean transformations where people were fired:* There are ardent fans of lean transformations, mostly the ones who kept their jobs. Previous transformations and consultant visits scare people. Be aware of it.

4 *The happy-clappy enterprise:* Some companies will not allow the use of the word "problem". There are no problems, only challenges. There are also environments where people go out of their way to be kind in order to create the perfect work environment. The effect of both is insidiously damaging. We need to acknowledge problems, and we need conflict in the right situations. Creativity is a process of problem, conflict, resolution.

5 *Autocracies:* There is a healthy respect for leadership, and then there is leadership that sets people up for failure because one or more senior leaders don't know how to lead change. We find that this is simply not worth calling out. You need leadership support, so work on the positive side of the OM and transformation design and be sure to come up with a project that is low cost, relatively fast and has clear benefits.

6 *Projects have gone wrong:* The company has a history of project overruns and budgets bloating. It puts somebody, somewhere on the defensive and a lot of the explanations you encounter are designed to justify poor work practices. The Lighthouse solution, (see Chapter 9) is specifically designed to overcome this, so avoid being drawn into negative judgments. It happens; you have an answer.

7 *Toxic people:* Finally, you will find toxic people. Often, they are the ones with all the answers and wonder why

others are not keeping up. They can also be people who've lost control of a set of projects, and their only recourse is to frustrate the people who could make genuine improvements and shift the blame to them. We always call out toxic people and advise leadership to get them out of an influential position quickly.

All in all, though, you will find that sensitivity to the impact of bad leadership, the rise of toxic people, the IT-Business divide, lean legacies, people treated as legacy and too little tension are all going to crop up.

The method we use to deal with these problems is first, to keep our ears wide open so we spot them, but without jumping to conclusions too early. We appraise the sponsor so that any political implications of those problems get an airing. Call out what you can, even if it makes you unpopular.

The tools you need

A shortlist

1 Empathy.

2 A questionnaire to fall back on in the perspectives stage (we provide some later as well as a fuller list online).

3 Visualisations of AS-IS and target operating models (use templates rather than starting from scratch. You will find these on *The Transformation Sprint* website).

4 The same goes for strategy analysis. We provide templates online.

5 Flashcards (A4), we will describe these later.

6 Visual collaboration spaces like MIRO or Mural.

7 In situ screens from Webex or Nureya backed by collaboration software.

8 And of course, Whiteboards, Post-Its and markers.

Prerequisites

We are assuming you have negotiated a charter with senior management for access and the outcomes. This should also include an understanding that you will be doing the work your way and the charter won't be changed mid-flow.

Secondly, you need that strong project sponsor, and it pays to take that person through your requirements before starting work.

You require that the first set of interviews, say the first ten are set up before you go live on Day 1 and that the schedule will continue to fill up, in consultation with you. Emphasise hourly breaks between interviews (more on that later).

You should also pass on a list of the documents you need before Day 1 so that they are available when you start (see Chapter 5).

Having an office set aside for the interviews is also critical.

The Playback date and final report date should also be set before Day 1.

Remember this, overleaf, is your timeline and you are about to enter Perspective Gathering, having already requested documentation for Analysis:

TABLE 3.1. The phases of a Transformation Sprint (again)

1	Perspective Gathering different perspectives	Interviews to uncover on the problems **(Day 1 onwards)**
2	Analysis	Market analysis and technical literature analysis **(Day 4 onwards)**
3	Issues Document	Logging the major issues **(Day 1 onwards)**
4	Describing the AS-IS and Future Operating Model	In draft form **(Day 12 onwards)**
5	Playback	To the executives and with prioritisation as a target **(Day 13 or 15)**
6	Lighthouse Outline Design	Days (16 -20)

Perspectives

In this chapter we are going to talk about how you gather information from people in the business. This is more or less happening from the day the project goes live, though you will have done your preparation work beforehand.

We'll cover the main objectives of the interviews we propose that you undertake. Why do these interviews? We will explain that, how to select interviewees, how to meet the challenges of interviewing and the interview process. We have included some sample questions too.

Objectives

In this first phase you will be collecting perspectives from people at every level of the firm. That means conducting interviews, cross referencing the interviews as you go, identifying key issues and cross-referencing these with documentation.

It is potentially complex but in this chapter we will explain who to interview, how to do the interviews, the challenges you'll face, how to build empathy with interviewees, what we are looking to discover in the interviews; and we will show some sample questions.

The interviews take place over the first 10 days and take 30 - 45 minutes each. But as we said earlier, this Phase overlaps with Phases 2 and 3. Already at this stage you must be pressing your sponsor for the documentation (see next chapter). We normally send a list before we start the sprint.

Nor do you need to conduct all of these before moving onto the executive playback session.

The playback session is partly there to create momentum. If you delay it, then you allow senior leaders off the hook, effectively communicating to them that delays are ok for leaders.

In perspective gathering our objective is to assess the flow of value through the organisation, including:

- The state of the operating model (the flow of value through from customers, marketing, business and IT and the state of these relationships, the impact of financing cycles, handovers, and ways of work - e.g scrum, SAFe, LeSS, design sprints, degrees of automation, etc).

- Where and how value originates and how effective is the innovation process.

- The impact of the corporate immune system on innovation.

- The degree to which revenues are being acquired through the exploitation of existing customers through known assets.

- Or the degree of dynamism, where value and revenues are being acquired through new activities (innovations in marketing. new proposition building, new products, services, service levels or features.

- Relationships with customers and markets, for example, the use of segmentation and dynamic segmentation.

- Where the organisation is disrupting or blocking the flow of value.

- How market conditions affect value discovery and value management.

- The impact of the resource mix: employees, contractors, offshore.

The interviews are designed to explore those issues.

The importance of perspectives.

At the outset, leaders can be cautious about staff being interviewed. There is a cultural shape to organisations that says leaders have the best insights. But we contend that organisations have conflicts that often reflect structural impediments. The conflict between people is real but it has its origins in systems that neither side can quite get a handle on.

It's also true to say that some employees have insights that could be of great value but they've never been given a voice.

There is also the fact to take into account that situations naturally have different perspectives.

A data scientist may see a problem quite differently from

an employee in customer care, who in turn will have a different perspective from an employee in logistics.

It is important to respect these differences. They give insights into OM breakdown.

For example, in an engagement with a subsidiary of a large multinational, we found several people who expressed frustration that projects were too large and typically overran. To overcome this problem, senior management had bought in a digital team as a complete unit and asked the team leader to use agile ways of working and spread the word.

Different perspectives are seen as a threat to the one real truth that is owned by senior management. You can win this argument by saying that just one novel perspective could save the company millions of dollars, so they see it as an opportunity not a threat.

To some degree, this was successful in that the company began launching its large projects before perfecting them. But that meant they were launching broken projects and this was being described as an agile way of working.

It led to a huge amount of senior time being spent on repairing the damage done by poor platform performance, because of an unexpectedly high customer complaint count.

Through interviews, however, we learned that the digital team was under-delivering. It was probably the least efficient digital team we have seen. There was no agility here.

The real problem can be summarised as:

1 Fundamentally a division between marketing and customer service created by poor platform integrations.

2 Digital team encouraging agility in inappropriate contexts, exacerbating that problem.

3 A need to define the OM around better data on markets and customers, which was largely overlooked because marketing were not seen as core to the transformation.

Interviews are a way of getting at these problems rather than taking management perspectives as a gospel.

Selecting interviewees

We ask senior managers to select the first round of interviewees and we ask for a cross-section.

We have found that some managers screen out "awkward customers" or those with a controversial point of view.

In the course of the first dozen interviews, we often get passed onto other people that interviewees think we must talk to. That way we get to the more controversial voices.

We have a schedule of questions we want to work through but we are never dogmatic about this. If the interview takes a detour that can have value too.

We are not aiming for any statistical inferences. This is pure qualitative research.

We also interview members of the senior management team.

Challenges with interviews

In general, people are willing and able to share their perspectives. However, two challenges arise.

Many staff have already been through a series of interviews with a consultancy. Those interviews tend to feed into a suite of KPIs. This might have happened with a consultancy like McKinsey.

The McKinsey KPI-set is impressive in its breadth but is focused on **compliance** with agile work practices.

There is nothing inherent in agile work practices that will provide higher value work. Agile is designed for faster work and, although the manifesto mentions VALUE, it implicitly defines it as removal of waste rather than a value-add.

To that extent, employees may feel they have already gone through a ritual that is designed to lead to cost-cutting and rule imposition.

They need to be reassured that this is different. Nobody's job or budget is at risk. It is all about uncovering THEIR perspective and feeding that into senior management discussions.

The second challenge is that people are often advocates for a particular group within the firm. There's no way around this other than to listen intently as you would with anybody in an adult conversation. However, when swapping notes with co-interviewers later, you can explore where the lobby groups have formed and what has caused them to form.

The interview process

We spend the first two weeks of a sprint discovering new perspectives on the types and sources of good and poor performance. We interview people at all levels and we dissect technical and strategy documents.

Most interviews are face to face, though post COVID19 that should be balanced against hygiene and safety concerns.

While we do between 30 and 45 interviews, our goal is to summarise them in real-time. That means one of us is typing as we interview and within hours we have extracted the most important points.

Deciding what is an important point is an interesting question of balanced judgment. People use the interviews to advocate for a cause. We are looking for signs that a background model is not working, so we have to resist the advocacy and look for the structural problem.

These are the areas we raise questions on:

- *Where and how value originates.* In most industries, the origins of value are changing, moving away from physical assets towards intangibles such as how consumers feel about a company or how they experience the interaction. Where is the firm on this journey?

- *The effectiveness of the business innovation process.* Is the company running a lab or incubator and do products, services or features successfully get into the organisation from there? Is the company running a lot of fail fast, fail cheap projects that are blocking the innovation funnel. Is there an effective test-and-learn process? How is failure dealt with?

- *Can we document the company's immune system type?*

  - *Tech-centric.* Companies heavy on technical expertise tend to have difficulty absorbing ideas that are dependent on intangibles such as experience.

  - *Data-centric.* Very data-centric companies have difficulty absorbing ideas that appear intuitive and untested.

  - *Scale-centric.* Large companies may block

innovations that do not have an obvious route to scale.

- *Channel-centric.* Companies with a long history of using sales channels struggle with ideas that need a direct relationship with end consumers.

- *Finance-centric.* Companies that need to move to a micro-transaction model may be struggling to convince the CFO office.

- *The flow of value.*

  - Whether value is static, in the sense of largely being acquired through the exploitation of existing customers through known assets

  - Or dynamic, therefore originating in new activities.

- *Segmentation and markets.* What are the main market segments it addresses? Query relationships with customers and attitudes towards the wider market. What segments does the company use to understand its market? How was the segmentation arrived at? Is there any use for example of dynamic segmentation?

- *Blockers.* Where is the organisation disrupting or blocking the flow of value.

- *Challenges of introducing process innovation.* Are they fixated on a traditional set of KPI's (Key Performance Indicators) that have become stale?

- *Value seeking behaviour.* What are the main marketing methods and channels; which technologies/platforms are used; is marketing work mainly agency driven or in-house? What is the status of these relationships (functional or not)? How do disruptive market conditions affect these value-seeking activities (is opportunity keenly perceived?

- **Resource mix.** The impact of the resource mix: employees: contractors: offshore: agencies?

- **Budget cycles and resource governance.** To what extent are annual budget cycles distorting behaviour and decision making? What is the scope for a more agile approach to finance?

Sample questions

Here are a subset of the types of questions used:

We ask questions across these categories:	• Value in goal definition and resource allocation (small steps)
	• Value-centred solution design and workflow (effective hierarchy and internal networking)
	• Value in Process Design (modeling and orchestration skills)
	• Pulse check (engagement and diversity)
	• Methodologies (Agility, Lean Six Sigma, Systems Thinking etc.)

TABLE 4.1. Categories of questions to probe on

We don't do multiple-choice questions because we prefer to be conversational but we do have a list in mind, as a reference point.

From the samples below you can see the kinds of concerns we have in our minds when opening a dialogue.

Questions on value-centred solution design and workflow (effective hierarchy and internal networking)	<ul><li>Are you well resourced to learn about new techniques to design solutions?</li><li>Or do you need more resources to keep up to date with the latest techniques?</li><li>Are you struggling with backlog issues or are there ways to stop the clock to ensure your solution designs are contextually appropriate?</li><li>Do leaders tend to lead the discussion or the design of solutions rather than coach you into discovering solutions?</li><li>Are you able to be diligent about setting goals for each of your sprints?</li><li>Are you equipped to assess the value of any feature you create?</li><li>Are you able to challenge business sponsors if you think work does not have enough value?</li><li>Typically do you get to work on a project end-to-end without interruption or is most of your work interrupted by the need to take on other tasks?</li><li>The handover of work from one team or department to another:<ul><li>Is minimal and not challenging at all;</li><li>Happens from time to time and has a manageable impact;</li><li>Is a major challenge for productivity.</li></ul></li></ul>

TABLE 4.2. Questions on value activities

Questions on goal alignment and resource allocation	• Do you feel that overall your work aligns well with what you know of the company's goals? • Do you have regular access to the end-users of your product/service or features? • Do you have a strong sense that your work creates success for the people using the outputs, the end-user? • Do you get regular show-and-tell opportunities so you refine your understanding of stakeholder needs? • How rigid would you say your ROI is? • Do you work in holistic teams? • Are you able to pivot out of wasteful work when it becomes obvious an idea is not going to fly?

TABLE 4.3. Questions on alignment

Some people feel that interviewing is difficult but it does become easier with practice and you will soon be able to spot patterns and to triangulate topics across the interviews (which you need to take note of). But one key technique is to be an active listener and ask open-ended questions, as any coach can tell you!

Analysis

In this chapter, we are going to describe Phase 2, which is largely about collating sufficient documentation to understand strategy, technical architecture, underlying handover problems, innovation practices such as value proposition building, market positioning and customer relationships. We'll also provide a sample template to help shortcut your analysis.

Objectives

Most companies in transformations generate huge amounts of paperwork. These will be presentations from consultants, strategy papers, workshop outputs, Project Management Office (PMO) progress reports outputs and so on. Very few of them are capable of reading, interpreting and acting on all the information in these documents. The quantity is too vast.

A Transformation Sprint doesn't want the luxury of detailed reading and analysis. We use the interviews to discover issues.

Alongside the interviews, the Transformation Sprint reviews the documentation but at sprint speed.

There are three objectives:

- Discover any striking new material that illustrates the pursuit of new value.

- Sanity check the interviews and see how the documentation segues with people's perspectives.

- Create a simplified representation of what it implies for the AS-IS or the target operating model.

Why are these important?

1 Does the documentation show any consistent messaging around creating new value? We have seen multiple transformations where there is no attempt to do anything different in the market or where customer value is not enlightened.

a Transformations become an end in themselves without changing how the company approaches market opportunity. For example, in one company we worked with, the emergent operating model was definitely platform and ecosystem centered. However, the company had no plan to disintermediate existing agents or convert them into a more dynamic force for delivering value. There needs to be some evidence that the company is going to reposition or is going to accelerate innovation or innovate in new ways.

b Often when companies talk about customer-centricity they mean acquiring more customers. There's nothing wrong with that but they don't change their perception of customers or what they can do for them. They don't get the idea of customer success.

If the answer to those questions is positive - they have new ways to innovate and intend repositioning - the chances are people will feel less dissatisfaction with the process.

As we've already said, transformation is often a cloak for firing people (retiring FTEs!). Staff get that and will resist it. In the playback session, it is important to reveal either or and to take a view on whether the transformation program is going to create new value discovery opportunities.

2 Sanity checking the interviews. Companies in transformation rarely do a thorough job of informing staff. It is important to glean from the interviews where interviewees think the company is heading. If the documentation and the interviews are at odds, then that is important for the playback.

3 Create a simplified view of the AS-IS and target operating model (with the help of your graphics expert). Very often transformations are set up as waterfall projects. They are big, clunky and value is years in the distance.

You can't overlook the fact that a firm wanting to be agile should not be setting up a multiyear transformation program.

The TOM will be hidden within reams of documentation and long consultant slide decks. That means nobody is going to be clear about the end state and that too is very valuable for the playback.

And, by looking into the documentation you can see the levels of complexity that the company uses to describe its journey and end state. The documentation will also show huge layers of complexity in core platforms. These

are the best arguments to scale back and skill up, which is the purpose of the Lighthouse.

The tasks are:

1 Log any clear intentions to innovate in new ways or to seek value in new ways.

2 Log any evidence of changing attitudes to customers and intermediaries.

3 Log system and core platform complexity.

4 Outline the AS-IS and TO-BE.

Documentation

It is important to have a thorough set of documents available, even though you won't be reading them in detail. Examples of the documents reviewed are listed overleaf:

TABLE 5.1. Types of documentation you need

Vision, mission and goals statements	Is one available? Are these elements coherent? Does it provide direction and concrete actions? For example, very often goals are stated as a set of KPIs rather than as a small set of priorities for the senior team.
Business Strategy	How much of a "grand plan" is it compared to how much "test-and-learn" has been designed in? How cost-reduction based rather than growth based?
Organisational structure	These are always out of date and will require validation.
Technical architecture	This will require a number of iterations before you understand it fully, so be sure to interview architects to help you.
Technology strategy	Very rarely will this artefact be up to date, so how much of a gap is there? Are they delivering on the stated objectives or are they too aspirational?
Operating model and handover processes between business and IT	More likely than not, this will not exist in paper form but it will come out (usually negatively) in the interviews.

Competitor analysis or SWOT presentations	We have found companies that look enviously at competitors without analysing their behaviours. Is there a succinct statement of your company's market position vis a vis change and competitors?
Social media analytics	Do you use one of the analytics suites like Sprinklr or Crimson Hexagon? What do they say about market positioning and fandom?
Market segmentation	Most segmentations are far too narrow and reflect the product range rather than market realities.
SEO data	Most to the point, does the company pay any attention to its visibility online?
Data strategy and data management	We still see companies with no data strategy and often replicated data activities. Is there a strategy? Is it going to get tied up in a data normalisation project? Or is there a small steps approach?
Operating model	Is the company explicit about this operating model or does it just talk about a target operating model (TOM)? Check the latter. If it runs into many pages of consultant speak, there is a problem.

Technical telltale signs and common issues to look out for

There are some common problems in technology infrastructure and services to look out for as you interpret the analysis and apply it.

Querying the following areas will provide a good indication of maturity:

1 The number of core platforms

Every organisation has numerous platforms, from analytical data warehouses to front-end digital platforms consisting of websites and apps. But it is worth focusing on what we call core platforms as these tend to offer the biggest transformation challenge.

A core platform is also known as a System of Record. There are other such systems - systems of differentiation, and systems of interaction. But these decline in complexity along the way. For example, systems of interaction are really digital front ends to the more problematic, tangle of core platforms in the background.

As another example, in a banking system current accounts and savings accounts would be associated with systems of record, those that log customer details such as name, address, and date of birth.

In the retail world, the core platform is likely to be built around a product catalogue (SKUs) and customer data.

Core platforms can also be those systems of interaction that interface directly with Systems of Record (for example, mobile or CRM). In essence, they are all systems that run the company.

In a digital transformation, the most common error made is to add a new front-end app or website to an existing set of core platforms.

This is where the first signs of conflict and frustration arise. Changes to the new digital front-ends can be made in minutes whereas the core platforms could still be on a monthly cadence, or longer. Look out for issues that arise in this "pace-layered" environment.

Your first sign of enterprise sophistication is the number of core platforms. One simple set of core platforms is ideal but it's unusual unless you are working with a startup.

Several core platforms that have grown over many years, or have been added to via mergers and acquisitions, are much more common.

The worst-case scenario that we have seen was 60 core platforms with significant replication and prolonged delivery times.

So, the first telltale sign is the number of core platforms. Part of the Playback to the senior leadership team contains the number of core platforms, the duplication and the conflicts.

2 Two-speed IT

Too many transformations focus on the digital customer experience but never tackle the core platforms on which those experiences depend.

In addition to the number of platforms, their age is also a factor. The oldest platform that we have encountered dates back to 1970. Unfortunately, this is not uncommon. A recent study in the US found that the Banking and Finance sector had the highest number of core platforms over 50 years old.

The critical issue here is the skills required to manage these old systems are in short supply. And this leads to the most common transformational error- two-speed IT. That means the current IT team receives no training to work with the new technology. Companies try to maintain their existing legacy delivery cadence by adding a new external team to build and deliver the digital front-ends.

You may have heard that some companies set up digital app factories. Great idea, but they alienate the current IT team who have the power, due to dependencies, to thwart the efforts of the new digital teams. That's another significant issue.

The telltale sign here is culture clashes between the current operating model teams versus future state teams.

3 Ways of working

One of the first indications of a failing transformation can be right in front of your eyes. And that can be the lack of visualisations in the office, no 'buzz' or atmosphere amongst the teams, too much dependence on the corporation's cultural messaging.

In our experience, the significant issues always lead to some toxic or micro-management behaviours within middle management. It's not uncommon to find that the 'team' has given up fighting against middle managers and is displaying passive aggression.

Calling out the toxic behaviour or management's lack of cultural awareness will help with the Lighthouse design. Later, we want these teams to co-create new ways of working and the associated agile methodology.

They will only do that if they feel management is listening to them.

4 *Vendors, suppliers, outsourcing and offshoring*

Understanding the key relationships and services offered among these groups is vital. Issues arise in these areas because of adversarial relationships stemming from leadership-driven contracts based on cost reduction rather than shared value.

Again, the mission here is to document, not judge, and base comments on best practices.

5 *Resources: people and platforms*

Another common issue you'll uncover within the AS-IS analysis will be the lack of resources to work on key initiatives.

However, the most significant issues arise from a lack of executive involvement in value management (hence the need for a portfolio wall) with many resources tied to the maintenance of old core platforms.

It's typical for executives to question the number of IT resources without any idea as to the cause of the issue, which can directly correlate to the number of platforms.

Resources in terms of platforms usually mean a contest between the computers and servers used to deliver products and services to customers, and the development and test environments used by IT staff.

A lack of development and test platforms is the telltale sign of two things:

- Overly complicated procedures involving bureaucratic IT staff in bullshit jobs, creating bottlenecks.

- The lack of Cloud services in the enterprise or who controls Cloud usage.

In the Playback, you can focus leaders on the potential lack of development productivity and poor quality of delivery to end customers.

6 *Processes and automation*

We emphasise data gathering at this stage and avoid going into solution mode. But it is worth ascertaining the amount of automation that exists for value delivery (continuous deployment, etc.) and the lead time between software development completion and deployment.

These two areas can provide a significant source of improvement within the Lighthouse Project by allowing the team to build deployment pipelines, automated testing and "people free" delivery mechanisms.

The telltale signs here are the lack of automation, the amount of process around delivery and the number of teams involved.

7 *Complex architecture*

An IT or systems architecture audit can help the Sprint. A strong starting point is to ask for a one-page view of the current architecture.

If that architecture cannot be drawn on A4 paper, without loss of insight, then complexity will be a given. An A0 piece of paper should sound alarm bells and if it has to be drawn on a plotter, this will signal the need for simplification and platform retirement candidates.

In the tables below we'll summarise some key issues in the technology analysis.

These issues will later be represented in the AS-IS state.

Research

Independent research about the organisation to identify opportunities and challenges.

- Portfolio of Work - review, in broad outline, the overall portfolio, especially in the transformation project.

- Peer Analysis - review major competitors including reviewing their social media presence and support.

- Markets - analyse transformation in the markets the company operates within.

- Growth Potential - assessing areas for continued growth v the need to explore new options.

- Leadership - backgrounds and skill sets of the leadership team.

- Sentiment - through the net promoter score or other sources such as Glassdoor and social media.

- Contact centres - observe activity in the call centres.

You can usefully summarise the information in this chapter with a red, amber, green table. The table below shows the principle as applied to the business analysis.

On **The Transformation Sprint** website we have provided 4 templates for participants in the Transformation Sprint training program. They can be used to analyse technology, business strategy, external interactions and processes.

ANALYSIS	RED FLAG
Business Strategy	Documents are over 12 months old and in multiple inordinately long slide decks
Transformation Strategy	Broad extent and large scale non-memorable
Transformation Performance	Misaligned leadership team and fragmented execution, clear ineffective hierarchy exposed through micromanagement
Consistency	Key strategy elements not reflected in actions in the transformation
Vision, Mission Goals	Unavailable or not coherent
Market Segmentation	Summary/ undetailed, reflects product range
Customer Centricity	Lip service, customer is still the target
Prior Consultancy Documents	Multiple consultancies, huge document depository

TABLE 5.2. Analytical template sample

AMBER ALERT	ALL IS GOOD
Strategy doesn't relate the AS IS - TO BE journey to market changes	Highly relevant to market changes - explicitly stated with route for iterating towards success
Manageable scope but signs of conflict emerging	Focused, iterative manageable with good learning practices
Alignment or execution is broken. Signs of dependency, over-complexity and conflict interfering with workflow	Strongly aligned and good execution with clear workflow
Middling consistency with some actions and strategy aligned	Actions strongly consistent with strategy
A mix of both	Well set out and influential on behaviour
Some detail but over-reliant on existing customer segmentation	Micro-segments, reflect emerging market needs
Desire expressed through actionable ideas for change	Customers engaged in reviews or other relevant actions
Extensive documentation	Ability to communicate plan on an A3

The Issues Document

In this chapter, we are going to talk about the Issues Document (drum roll!). We create an Issues Document to set out the main issues a company faces during its transformation (or once it has become blocked).

In truth, these tend to be standard across companies, but you need to find the top ten, and you need to assess their impact and order of importance. We will review the relationship between this critical document and the Perspectives and Analysis phases. We will also relate it to the overall outcomes of the Sprint. We will provide you some sample issues to guide your analysis. Finally, we will briefly explain what use you will make of the document.

Relationship to perspectives

Earlier, we emphasised that you are promising to identify the top ten issues that are holding a transformation back. These tend to point to underlying structural problems

that need to be solved. We log those issues in an Issues Document. We share that document from early on with the project sponsor.

The objectives of the document are:

- To capture issues early, from interviews and documentation, before they are either forgotten or overlooked.

- To make sure the issue log is complete and comprehensive by using it as the sole repository of issues we uncover.

- To help other interviewees to cross-reference their insights by adding to the log.

- To start the thought process on what to prioritise and what viable solutions the document suggests.

- To give the sponsor insights into issues arising so she can point up any political sensitivity that might arise.

- To make sure we build the overall enterprise issues' profile quickly.

- To create the main Playback exercise (see Playback!).

We create an Issues Document from Day 1 onwards, as soon as interviews start. This is usually a shared doc, that is to say, shared at least with the project sponsor. You can use Google docs for this.

We don't aim to produce a report that we hand over. This is a sprint, so we like to keep the momentum going. That means we begin, immediately, to list out the top 10 issues that are emerging from the interviews and literature review.

We also use a very iterative approach, as shown overleaf:

DIAGRAM 6.1. The iterative loop of work

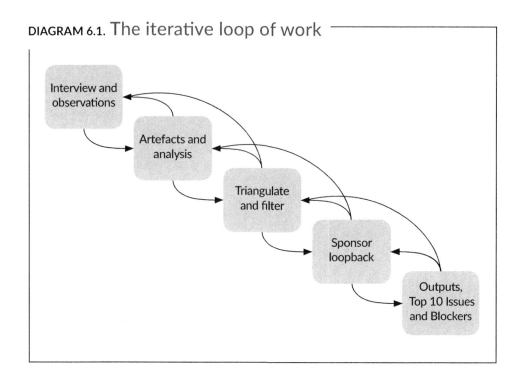

The interviews and observations that we make will change as we review the document artefacts that are guiding the company's transformation. We transpose the issues that arise in them into one single document, the Issues Document. We review interviews to see how many people, and which people, have made similar points, say about a toxic part of the company.

It's often the case that the accusation of toxicity comes from people who themselves have something to hide, so we have to filter out self-serving messages. The self-serving nature of perspectives is understandable and common but something to guard against.

The sponsor is often a useful source of advice on this triangulation and filtering process (checking in on the perspective gathering, understanding from who the key

issues are coming). He or she is also useful for alerting the Sprint team to problems that will not go down well politically and helping to find the right way to frame the issues. Generally, we end up with far too many issues, so we iterate back over the documents and interviews to determine which ones are holding back change. That might mean, for example, that a particularly messy handover is deprecated in the Issues Document because it is a symptom of a larger systems problem.

All of this is subjective to a degree but backed by lots of perspective gathering and a desire to be sure that the issues reflect an operating model problem, not just a day-to-day grievance or conflict.

Purpose of the document

The purpose of the Issues Document is to simplify. When you do interviews, you find people have many varied explanations for what is going on. Often your role is almost like a therapist. People are grateful for the opportunity to talk.

That can make for quite complex explanations too. You have to drive hard to simplify.

Issues can usually be grouped as the document grows. For example, if various problems seem to be related to handovers, then handovers become a critical issue.

Number and types of issues

That list might grow to 15 or 20 as we proceed. We whittle that down as we get near to the Playback. It can easily be the case that issues drop out at this stage, yet assume more importance after Playback.

Some points to bear in mind:

1 Try not to let the list grow too long - it is a critical issues list (ten is optimal) and grouping will help you zone in on the most important ones. You might even use frequency of mention (by interviewees) as an indicator of importance. The resource or financial impact of the issues will also be the key. It is essential to be on the lookout for issues that point to an underlying problem.

2 To that end try to ensure that the issues have an operating model context i.e.

   a They expose structural fault lines - a classic example of which would be the addition of digital front end technology to a tangle of outdated platforms;

   b They expose misalignment - a classic would be companies that try to be customer-centric while doing little to engage customers in new ways;

   c They illustrate inconsistencies and inefficiencies in ways of working - a classic example would be no explicit PMO control of or insight into workstream dependencies;

   d They point to significant recurring failures, particularly big project failures and overruns;

   e They point to a missing competence or competency that the company believes it has but, in reality, is weak on.

3 In that context, in your HR interviews, test out the insight that the HR team has around new and emerging skills.

4 Build the issues from the interviews but triangulate. Never take one interviewee's opinion as gospel.

5 Add in from documentation.

We often see that issues stemming from broken and blocked transformations are created by poor OM design and that this lies behind the inability to transition people and their styles of work.

Release

At most, release to the sponsor, and only the sponsor, from Day 2 onward.

Make the claim that we can deliver value frequently, a really substantial one. Ultimately the firm needs to work in much more value-seeking ways on a much shorter fuse. Announce the pace and stick to it.

Make it an active document where sponsors can see dynamic updates. But don't make it too widely available, or you will activate the immune system. The sponsor and her team are enough.

Get the sponsor to annotate. The sponsor's views are vital to winning acceptance for the prioritisation process.

Use and format of Issues Document

The Issues Document is going to become a crucial part of kicking off the executive Playback workshop. In the Playback, we use flashcards on the wall that highlight the top 10 - 12 issues. We then ask executives to place a Post-It note under the five issues that are most pressing in their workday. Overleaf (see table 6.1.) we have summarised typical issues that arise and we've provided a longer explanation in the pages that follow.

TABLE 6.1. A non-exhaustive summary of critical issues that arise

	The Problem	In Brief
1	Vision, mission goals unarticulated	You'd be surprised how many leadership teams don't do the basics
2	Customer-centricity	Companies want to do it but don't know-how, yet convince themselves they do
3	Market segmentation	Companies understand the market and customers through their product range rather than through insight. It puts the brakes on change
4	Handovers	Work is a collaborative experience, but handing work over from one section to another routinely causes misunderstanding and inefficiency
5	Core platform incompatibility and age	Company has too much legacy business sustained by too many platforms that prevent progress
6	Poor resource allocation	Lack of a central, visible project register
7	Poor value discovery	Companies can get overwhelmed by fail fast and fail cheap projects or iterations that go too far into development before their lack of value is acknowledged
8	Major projects	A long history of failure reduces morale and creates fear

9	Ineffective hierarchy	Senior leaders who micromanage and believe they can bully people into changing, added to leadership fixating on minor operational detail
10	Decision-making challenges	Senior leaders come from different industry backgrounds and try to apply inappropriate lessons from the past
11	Lack of staff churn	Complacency and pleasantness keep the company on an even keel but headed nowhere
12	Customer journey design problems	Inability to envision the customer journey
13	Discount wars	Using price and discounts as the first weapon of choice
14	Leaders as showmen	Dominating meetings and reducing the scope for collaboration because of ego
15	Bound by the past	No valid future of business exploration or remodelling skills
16	FTE reduction and contractor increases	Making decisions based on FTE reduction rather than taking cost decisions based on where real waste lies
17	Risk management	A lack of alignment between agile teams and the slower practices or steps required by risk or security teams
18	Risk controls	Long risk registers, with numerous red risks which have remained unresolved for months if not years

That means your issue has to have a Twitter-like summary.

Below we provide you with a slightly longer explanation. You can use this in conjunction with the assessment of the AS-IS state that we have laid out in Chapter 7. Remember, all of this work is iterative.

1 *Vision, mission, goals.* Are the vision and mission driving prioritisation in the leadership team? Is there any prioritisation? "Vision and mission are irrelevant to my work," was one middle manager's verdict in a company we worked with. Too many projects start. Too many drag on for too long. In the meantime, there is insufficient value-based selection going on. That's because there is too little strategic prioritisation driven by vision and mission as leaders claim they are too busy with crisis management.

2 *The customer-centricity problem.* Customer relations for incumbents can be as simple a marketing budget, backed by a set of call centres (usually outsourced) to deal with complaints or to explain new deals. And a billing system, backed by credit control. That leaves a vacuum where customer care strategies should be winning over customers and reducing churn. The problem often is that they do not perceive market conditions from the customers' point of view. The customer represents the potential for an upsell or a cross-sell. Having a strategy for customers that makes them less of a target and more of a partner is critical but rarer than it should be.

    Investment tends to be in systems that allow the firm to capture more customers data or normalise the

data they have. There is nothing intrinsically wrong in this, but knowing what customers buy is not being customer-centric. There are many facets to that, including how you segment your market.

3 **The segmentation problem.** The customer-centric problem extends to areas such as market segmentation. The company will segment, but they segment according to their existing customer base, and they tend to segment based on responsiveness to their own product line or what they perceive as customer lifetime value. That gives them segmentations such as Top 10% based on customer spend (or some other spend threshold). That's useful if you know how to move the percentile 11-20% up, so the information is valuable. Or it will be a segmentation based on product categories.

Really, this is all historical information whereas you want a segmentation to be predictive about all customers, yours and our competitors. The current lifetime value is not where your focus should be. You want to know the future lifetime value for a new and sometimes undeveloped set of services.

4 **Handovers.** The development of an agile work methodology is often confined to some parts of IT and does not extend to the business side. It encourages business to send more work to IT, but with no apparent value-discovery process. Companies know how to spin up new propositions and then iterate to a new product. But that puts far too much pressure on IT. Much of the work is of dubious value. IT will manage its backlog conservatively in response, a classic example of the IT-business divide. No holistic (IT/business) teams is a sign to be looking out for.

5 *Core platform problems.* A company's internal complexity increases as they struggle to establish the systems that would allow them to function in a more digital culture. It can be, for example, that companies struggle to onboard customers because they have dual, digital and analogue systems. Often the complexity stems from an unwillingness to retire old lines of business and old systems.

When an incumbent becomes more digital and wins new business, its campaigns may have been conceived rapidly in response to marketing initiatives from nimble competitors. Ironically, winning new customers puts pressure on the customer service function in companies in transformation.

Typical solutions include a re-platforming of their core systems or the addition of yet more systems (and with it the development of a large contractor workforce to support the fight against technical debt and workstream dependency problems). Look out, talk of two-speed IT, a large contractor workforce, the presence of vendor employees in the building, a PMO under strain, and over-complex workstream visualisations.

Among the other common things we see are duplication in core platforms due to mergers and acquisitions) and a lack of investment or ability to collapse those platforms together. The business is usually great at the "A" and either not able or willing to do the "M".

6 *Poor resource allocation.* Too many projects with not enough time spent on the discovery of their real value; it means the business is pushing too many

projects into development and production without a clear idea of their value.

7   *Poor value discovery techniques.* Usually stems from the presence of ideation platforms, hackathons and other methods that create a profusion of ideas that then need complex evaluations. Companies need real value discovery mechanisms.

8   *The major projects problem.* At some point, a company will realise that its digital transformation has become a succession of failed projects. It takes on grand new plans and fails to deliver. There's no great surprise here. The whole rationale of scrum and agile is to move away from ambitious plans. They don't work well. All these new capabilities: data, marketing, customer centricity, responsiveness, intelligence and insight, rely on good system choices. But many companies are not making choices at all. They have a tangle of old systems that they have been trying to make good. Projects have to endure an infrastructure that doesn't work.

9   *The ineffective hierarchy problem.* Many of these problems make it very difficult for a leadership team to hang together. They expose themselves to career risk. Not untypically they, or the CEO, will begin to micromanage. The belief that all problems can be traced back to unwillingness and incompetence takes hold. The answer is to bash a few heads together. Alternatively, they get dragged into day-to-day operational problems and don't lift their heads to see what is on the horizon.

10 *Decision-making challenges.* Senior leadership team members are from multiple different industries and

are trying to replicate what they know and what worked for them in the past. That means they often make decisions based on what they did in their last post. They also tend to delegate decisions, so they avoid blame.

11 **Lack of staff churn.** Cosy environments contribute to lethargy, orienting the business around older ideas and solutions. Staff turnover is healthy, helping to bring in new ideas, more energy and the opportunity for advancement. The undemanding work environment means everybody is trying to keep the peace and that can signal other problems, such as an unstated belief that the company is going nowhere so just don't rock the boat, pick up the pay cheque and wait for the holidays.

12 **Customer journey know-how is way too limited.** Customer journey mapping is often outdated. A tendency to see the company's own process as the journey is problematic. It leads to designs that try to force customers into the company's way of doing things or incentivising them with discounts. Digital experience is an offline and online one, and learning how to carry people across the digital and physical experience boundaries is an integral part of journey planning.

13 **Discount wars.** The company's reflex reaction to changes in the market is to discount. Insufficient data to know whether customers acquired through discounting pay back over a life cycle. Customer-centric issues: what is the real cost of customer acquisition; what about word-of-mouth strategies and community? No practical focusing on growth

segments/needs/product. The reflex market position is to discount!

14 *Leaders as showmen.* Predominantly male leadership teams use their positions to showboat in meetings, meaning younger staff get no say but also no input and no opportunity to learn. It has a tendency to create a permission-seeking culture.

15 *Bound by the past.* Some companies do away with strategy or the future-of-business unit. It means future exploration and new opportunity get squeezed into a dysfunctional environment where they cannot prosper. Executives seem bound by today's commoditisation and exploiting the current business model. However, a Future of Business unit could explore strategies to lift the stress of competition, price wars and the future of energy.

16 *FTE reduction and contractor increases.* Companies typically have a headcount reduction program. Equally typically, they are usually hiring contractors. This oddity is a budgetary issue, but it cleans out the people who might have long term loyalty and replaces them with people whose priority is to make the work last. It's a significant cause of passive aggression, and it also signals a lack of workstream planning as more bodies get hired to do less work!

The purpose of this summary is to underline three points:

1 The first is that many of the problems we encounter are entirely predictable. Within a range of 15 - 25 such issues, you can probably describe the dysfunctionality of most companies.

2 The second is that the perspective gathering gives you the context that allows you to describe the significant impediments to change.

3 And third, because the problems are predictable, so too are the answers.

Translating issue narratives into a decision exercise

We take these issues and create flashcards out of them (use slides in a remote context) for executive Playback. The purpose of the flashcards will be explained in more detail when we discuss the Playback workshop. Suffice to say for now that you want to create a set of statements that are clear and unambiguous. You will be asking leaders, in effect, to vote on which most nearly meets their own views of the underlying problems.

State the ten issues like this (think of them as Tweets):

Flashcard 1: Day to day activity is all about firefighting, rather than setting priorities.

Flashcard 2: Our industry needs to catch up with best practice elsewhere.

Flashcard 3: We're in a race to the bottom but can't change the status quo.

Flashcard 4: Our ability to set priorities is squeezed out by managing the fallout from big project problems.

Flashcard 5: Teams are too siloed, though in the leadership team we collaborate well.

Flashcard 6: We are losing the fight between innovation and stability.

With these issues translated into Flashcards, you have a crucial component of the Playback session in place. We advise continuing to revise the cards to get the word count down and to remove ambiguity.

Transformation and the Operating Model

We are now going to take a deeper dive into operating models. We want to clarify our proposition that generative operating models are better than non-generative target operating models. We need to define operating models, and we choose to do this through activities rather than structures. We'll explain that too.

We want you to come out of the other end of this chapter with a thorough understanding of the OM and its place in transformation programs. Therefore, we also need to review what goes wrong in operating models, as well as how we might describe the current status of a model and the clues we can pick up to explain any model that's emerging.

By looking at the OM, we can also identify faultlines that are emerging in the company's capability set, its technology base and its processes. That will lead us to describe future operating models and how to visualise these ready to playback to management.

Target and generative operating models

Most companies need to evolve their operating model (OM). The purpose of a transformation is to design and transition to the new OM, though the design is often overlooked.

We find quite a lot of confusion around the topic of operating models too.

In short, companies are unclear as to:

- What an operating model comprises.
- What their existing operating model is.
- And the nature of their future operating model.

Suppose the purpose of a transformation is to design and switch from one operating model to another. In that case, the doubt and uncertainty around these three factors is a significant cause of the breakdown.

In our experience, companies need what we call a "generative" operating model.

That term generative can be challenging to grasp but think of it as having the skills to generate new operating model designs. We argue that the most critical objective for a company in a transformation is to have the skills to create new target operating model designs that are generative in nature and then manage the corresponding transitions.

OM design is a specialised skill, based on:

- A thorough understanding of existing OM weaknesses.
- The needs of the marketplace.
- And the design of a future OM that helps generate new structures and enables rapid adaptation to market changes.

You can bring much clarity to this situation through the Transformation Sprint process.

Describing the operating model

Generally speaking, the OM is a set of rules (formal and informal), relationships and systems that enable the discovery of value and its management and delivery to customers through a sequence of value-adding and support activity.

It is not an organisational structure. For a long time, the concept of an operating model drew on Michael Porter's classic book Competitive Advantage. It looked something like this:

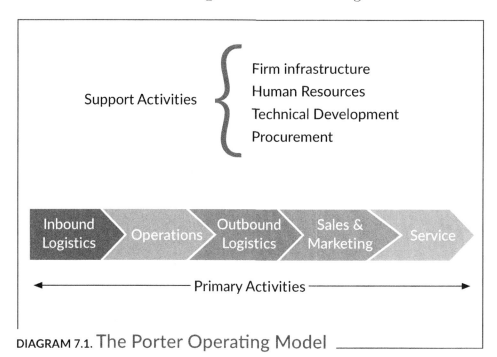

DIAGRAM 7.1. The Porter Operating Model

You'll notice the value-adding primary activities on the horizontal plane. In Porter's schema, they related closely to competitive advantage.

These ideas were valuable, indeed foundational, until recently.

Digital technology, however, has changed how value is created and distributed. For example, it is possible to conjure up products and services with no preceding value chain and no raw materials, making it possible to create multiple versions of a service at no extra cost (the so-called zero-marginal cost issue).

We now need to take a different view of the operating model. We prefer to break down the idea of a "model", with its connotation of a fixed structure, and recreate it as "activities", giving a greater sense of dynamism. For example:

- Formal and informal rules are really about the culture of an organisation. They speak to how free people are to explore value or to challenge work in progress. Alternatively, how constrained they are.

- Relationships are how parts of an organisation hand work on to other parts or receive and export work to partner organisations. More often than not, the most relevant set of rules (or governance principles) shape the relationship between the business (marketing, operations, finance, distribution, etc.) and the IT department.

- There are other aspects to this, of course. The handover in customer care from marketing to operations would be another critical source of friction or advantage, depending on how well the company manages these intersection points, an area not covered by Porter.

You may remember the diagram overleaf from earlier. These are the activities we think of as essential to the generative OM.

1 **Value discovery** is a critical innovation activity. It concerns innovation but not just innovation around

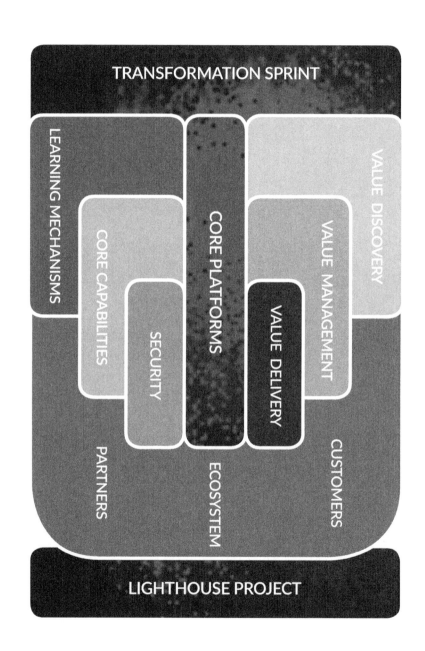

DIAGRAM 7.2. A generative operating model and change framework

TRANSFORMATION SPRINT

LEARNING MECHANISMS

CORE CAPABILITIES

SECURITY

CORE PLATFORMS

VALUE DELIVERY

VALUE MANAGEMENT

VALUE DISCOVERY

PARTNERS

ECOSYSTEM

CUSTOMERS

LIGHTHOUSE PROJECT

new products or services. Innovating the process, or innovating the operating model, and innovating relationships are equally meaningful. Traditionally, the innovation governance structure required new projects to go through a series of stage-gates as projects developed. This slowed innovation down. Companies have weeded gating systems out in favour of fail-fast, fail-cheap iterations, with the result that many innovation programs are now too light on direction and put too much pressure on IT resources. Some rebalancing is needed.

2 **Value management** is a critically overlooked factor, too. Many companies have a habit of destroying value and creating waste. That is ironic, we know. So how do they do it? By having immune systems resistant to change, by adding more and more new products and processes without retiring the old ones, and by not adhering to their own stated goals. There is also a lack of leadership involvement in the company's portfolio of work. Senior leaders think they know what teams are working on but in reality they don't, which often comes as a surprise to them when they see it visualised.

3 **Value delivery** is the ways of working that get value from discovery to the customer in the shape of a new product or service. Generally speaking, we think of value delivery as what takes place in the IT shop, and there, ways of work have been changed by a variety of agile frameworks and by new tools and techniques.

4 **Learning mechanisms** are often notable by their absence. Being good at all the skills that make up a competitive company implies that you have robust learning mechanisms. Most companies don't have

these. And they tend to reduce headcount frequently and in the process get rid of accumulated wisdom.

5 *Core capabilities* should be how you build the future. You also need to master new core capabilities as they emerge as a source of competitive advantage. Generally speaking, there is a war for talent for many mainstream skills, but it is much more intense for people who are capable of self-directed learning on new tasks and new needs.

6 *Cyber agility* is an up and coming pillar of how companies function. As businesses become more open (through mechanisms like APIs, broader partnership ecosystems, and remote work), they become more vulnerable to cyber attack. Protecting your business is now a growing priority and a potential source of advantage.

7 *Ecosystems* are the new orange. Crucially, we have also seen the gradual breakdown of company barriers over the past two decades, to the point where the operating model has to embrace the management of external environments or ecosystems.

8 *Customer-centricity* is an ambition in most companies. However, we often hear executives say, we would like to be more customer-centric but don't know how. The fact is that customers are a healthy source of innovation and an essential resource for insight. They are participants in your business. Look at Amazon and its reviewing system. The company stands or falls by customer participation.

9 *Core platforms* are a source of constant change and yet anchor companies in the past. Systems such

as IT platforms, billing and accounting systems are subject to continuous innovation and improvement by vendors, often at a very granular level, and have also enjoyed rapidly changing ways of working (for example combining development and operations - DevOps).

Very often, there is a core set of platforms and systems that are difficult to manage, even with the latest techniques. They might be a collection of platforms that date back 40 years or more. They are fundamentally incompatible. The main activity around them is their management and gradual upgrade.

Those, roughly speaking, are the elements of a generative OM based on activities. The generative concept gives you a framework for querying the AS-IS and future OM based on what is happening rather than being based on a structure. It also allows you to focus on priority activities.

What goes wrong in operating models?

A classic case of operating model transformation occurred when companies began to outsource more of their component production and assembly to their supply chains. At one point, companies produced all or most components in a product. Then they moved to assembly and began to use externally manufactured specialist components.

In the 1980s, this became a global movement that coincided with business process outsourcing. The two together, along with the introduction of Enterprise Resource Planning (ERP), radically altered company operating models.

Another critical change in OM occurred when companies moved away from old waterfall software development to more agile work practices.

That represented a transition from large, multi-year software projects that would deliver a new platform or similar substantial outcome every three years (say), to a series of smaller projects or sprints. These sprints had the opportunity to pivot regularly if the requirement of a project didn't seem achievable or somehow did not meet customer needs.

Agile may seem like an example of a target operating model. It should render large requirements as small projects that can pivot, and organise around smaller teams and a new hierarchy. Many claims are made for its influence. But it is at best it is only a subset of rules and relationships in a firm.

The problem is that it does not address enough of the critical challenges that arise with waterfall. It is an incomplete operating model, which is why we developed Lighthouse Thinking. Points of omission include:

The handover: Problems often arose because the handover process from business to IT was ill-conceived. Business sponsors and their teams would create a requirements document and then leave IT to execute it. Requirements documents could be very long, and very demanding, with little appreciation of the resources they would absorb or the project dependencies they would create.

The practice of the business creating the specification and handing it over has not gone away. Therefore handover conflicts remain.

Lack of upstream value analysis: Lean practices push too many projects into the innovation funnel. This comes on top of changes in business models, the introduction

of new technologies like AI/ML, and a much bigger regulatory requirement for most companies. The result is that teams context-switch between these initiatives too often. They become less efficient but, worse, are often working on projects with no proven value.

Dependencies: In the presence of weak innovation governance, many companies push too many projects into the flow of work, creating confusion and extended wait-times as teams wait for a deliverable from another part of a program. This gets exacerbated when executing a transformation program at the same time as managing projects in business-as-usual.

Customer-centricity and data: There is abundant data around that might be useful in making decisions about markets and internal processes or, indeed, partnership relationships. Not many companies can access this data, even though they own it! Very often, that means they do not leap into becoming genuinely customer-centric. Their decision models remain too centred on their own processes.

Although companies feel that going agile is a significant OM transformation, it can be a mistaken belief.

Agile is not an OM in reality. It needs much supplementing in terms of new value discovery techniques, value management, new systems, and new relationships. However, it is a start. Companies are right to embrace it but should see it as first base in the broader remodelling exercise.

Describing the AS-IS in outline

In our view, AS-IS states are best described through the underlying support technology as it flows out from strategy.

We will describe that below. The point we need to get to is a graphical representation of the AS-IS state. It needs to be simple so that people can share insights.

To do this, we prefer to use a set of concentric circles representing different activities.

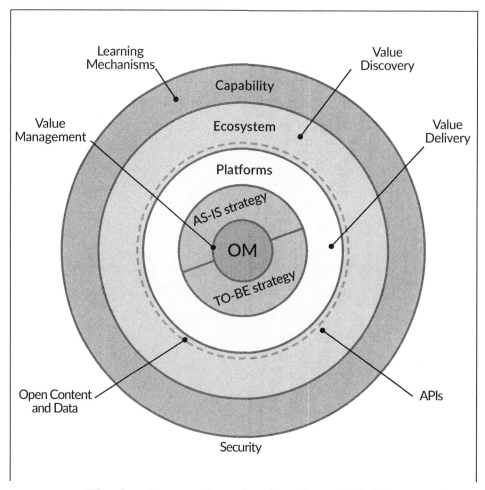

DIAGRAM 7.3 The basic template for logging OM failure points

In the diagram opposite we are representing the various activities that go into operating models. At the centre is the OM. Around it is strategy. Very often, when companies are in transition, they have two or more strategies that shape their objectives. They also make investment decisions that support different strategies, sometimes without being aware of the disparity. We will give an example of this below.

To a degree, it is normal and to be expected. That's what the change is all about. The problems arise when it is not sufficiently transparent and conscious.

Around the inner strategy circle in the diagram are the technology platforms that the company is using to deliver the strategy. The next circle around that represents the ecosystem of partners and internal relationships. And the final ring is made up of capabilities that the company needs but may not have.

This is a straightforward representation of multiple interrelated factors.

You will see the lines reaching into the circles that indicate where activities such as learning mechanisms, API connections, value discovery and so on take place.

It might seem more intuitive to draw up an AS-IS through specific functions such as inbound logistics, production, marketing, distribution, support services, etcetera. However, all this gives you is an organisational chart.

Businesses are much more dynamic than org charts. They consist of decades worth of technology, and incompatible processes that co-exist, along with rules, assumptions, relationships that often work imperfectly. These operational elements will have malfunctions. They will not always work well together.

We need to capture some of that dynamism in the interviews and then draw it out.

In the next diagram, you see the OM of a company that is running three different strategies. You might ask why it would do that? The answer is, it is a fact of transformation and a reason why they are hard to get right.

In this case, the company has a conventional business that operates through bricks and mortar intermediaries. It is coming from a B2B background. It might need to move to a B2C market position or something of a hybrid model (B2B2C).

Because of its skills in building relationships with large enterprises (B2B), it initially deploys its new operating model as a service to digital channels (such as websites and mobile networks). In this digital operating model, it could go direct to customers, though it chooses not to.

It also has a platform and ecosystem strategy. Its leaders half believe that there is scope to corral much smaller intermediaries and scale its business by creating a large class of independent apps' developers who can reach end customers on its behalf.

Here's how that looks at the outset. We have filled in the strategy segments in the diagram opposite.

DIAGRAM 7.4. A draft operating model with strategy logged

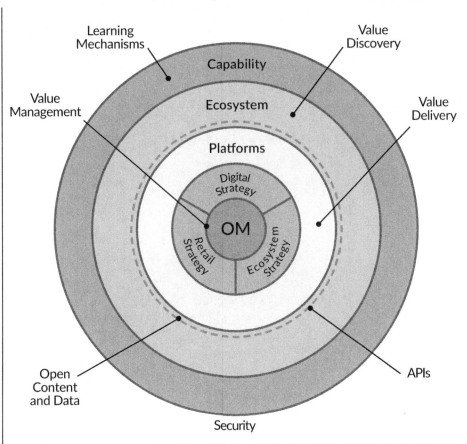

You can use simple diagrams like this to highlight where problems or fault lines exist. For example, there will inevitably be fault lines around the infrastructure and end-user platforms. We can now step through a few of those fault line analyses.

Finding the fault lines in capabilities

In this next diagram, we have created hotspots where serious problems exist. You will also notice that the chart is more complete than the previous one. What we then can do is illustrate those hotspots.

Here we have filled out the capabilities a company should have if it is serious about its digital future (the list could be longer, of course!).

DIAGRAM 7.5. A draft OM with platforms and capabilities logged

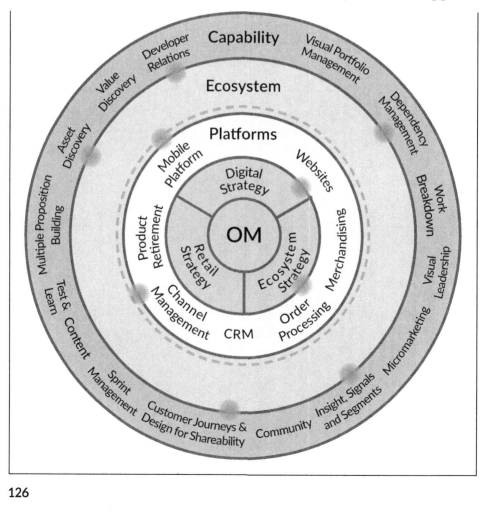

In this case, the company has underinvested in its digital and ecosystem platforms. In reality, it had spent vast amounts of money on them. In prioritising the traditional business, however, much of that work was incomplete and indeed wasted, as leaders repeatedly dragged teams over from digital and ecosystems to retail (the conventional business). Context switching of this type plays havoc with software development quality and easily doubles the cost of every aspect of work.

That also led to its developer relations program being dead in the water, along with its independent channels. There simply were not enough time and resources to give to these critical new operating choices.

Being so intent on sustaining its legacy business, it went through various attempts to go digital and go open, each time leaving assets behind that never got used. This asset drop out is another source of waste, and yet it is ubiquitous. Companies that are transitioning without the right OM design skills will always default back to the traditional business. And that often means taking a run at change in digital and in ecosystems but pulling back and leaving assets behind.

Finally, this company's customer journey mapping capability was underdeveloped, making mobile and other digital UI quite weak. The impact of that was to reduce the effectiveness of digital, especially mobile, channels, as reflected in its all-out discount pricing (we often see discounting as a default tactic when companies haven't thought through the customer journey).

The red dots identify these fault lines in the diagram. What we have provided on the template (see the following chart, too) is a list of potential new capabilities. You can assess a company's operating model partly by referring to these. Many of these capabilities will be missing because HR is not focused on hiring for tomorrow's business.

We ask questions like: Do they have community development and management capabilities? Do they develop new business ideas with a test-and-learn strategy? Do they use visual mechanisms to communicate or are communications focused on meetings and documents? In the innovation sphere, do they conduct asset discovery activities, or do they always rely on launching new lean-iteration or fail-fast, fail-cheap cheap projects? Can we pick up any clues on the asset drop out rate?

Finding the fault lines through the ecosystem

You can also assess their strengths and weaknesses in ecosystem development (see diagram opposite). We have filled in some sample ecosystem members, but there will be others. Companies that rely on formal partnerships tend not to have moved very far along the road to digital.

End users/customers should be part of the ecosystem, not just as people who attend focus groups. They should be part of a recognisable community that is active around the company's products and services.

You can use these concentric circles to grow a better awareness of OM fault lines. We will be improving and developing them over time and would appreciate your input.

You can annotate any part of the diagram to bring out other issues. For example, there were severe handover problems in one organisation that were costing the organisation very dearly because each had an impact on the customer experience.

That faultline ran between the Customer Relationship Management (CRM) system and Marketing platforms such as customer loyalty. Customer support had effectively hijacked the CRM, leaving marketers to seek permission to access data for pricing campaigns.

We can represent that by drawing lines out from those to platforms and annotating the problem.

DIAGRAM 7.4. A draft OM with platforms and ecosystems logged

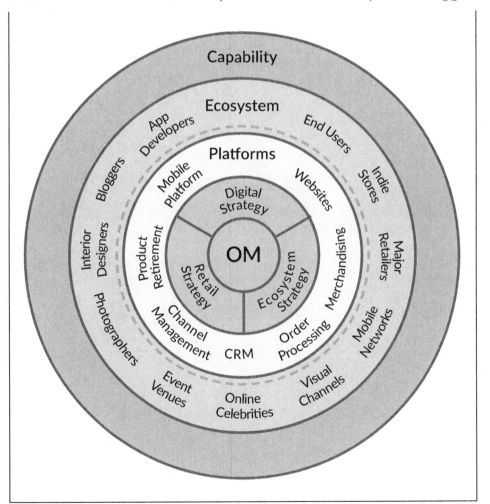

Technical and handover fault lines

Underneath the neat picture of a circle of core platforms, there will be a stack of overlapping, duplicated and replicated systems that have been around for a long time.

Practically every company on earth suffers some technical debt or some dysfunction in systems and ways of working around them. It is inevitable. Problems arise when leaders don't deal with legacy issues.

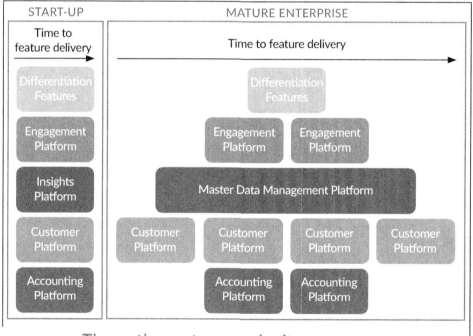

DIAGRAM 7.5. The pathway to complexity

This is partly an efficiency problem. But it is also a competency issue. A company can invest enormous resources over a long period trying to patch legacy systems together. We also see this in the increasing use of Robotic Process Automation (RPA) linking legacy platforms together for short term productivity gains.

This kicks the simplification problem down the road but much of the dysfunction is still there. Alternatively, the company can do the right thing and start retiring those parts that are causing the most problems. You can assess this through the interviews.

The target operating model

Entrepreneurs and consultants have designed several new operating models over recent years.

In our view, these are fixed destination points and potentially work against the principle of being generative. But once again, they are a start.

They include the Spotify Model, SAFe, Platforms and Ecosystems, the Data-driven Operating Model, the Digital Business Operating System and indeed Flow. Flow is the least prescriptive of any of these.

Examples of new operating models

- **The Spotify Model** has also been called the Spotify Tribe Engineering Model. This is a model for scaling agile teams. Team members belong to different autonomous units called Squads (6-12 person independent teams), Squads ladder up into Tribes or groups working on the same feature area, Chapters (horizontal subject experts), Guilds (informal groupings around a topic)). It is a sophisticated framework for scaling and augmenting agile scrum practices.

- **SAFe** is also a scaled agile framework but based around value streams. Teams curate value streams through scrum practices. SAFe has an extensive set of rules for how work should be carried out and supervised.

These rules have made it seem like a return to old waterfall practices.

- *Platforms and ecosystems* are two distinct sets of practices that often coincide. Companies like Netflix organise around internal platforms (billing platform, data platforms, delivery platform, device platforms and so on). Each platform has a specialist team. However, some teams specialise in areas such as marketing. Therefore, the marketing team might want to collaborate with the billing platform team to create new opportunities through billing communications. Light guardrails, rather than rules and processes, govern this matrix of activities. Similarly, Amazon began to focus on self-service platforms (Amazon Web Services, AWS, Fulfilled by Amazon, FBA and Kindle Direct Publishing, KDP) from about 2007 and then the data capabilities that power these, from about 2010. They have recently released more platform plays such as Handmade and Amazon Business.

- *Pure ecosystem models:* because of the amount of platform-as-a-service offering out there, it is not necessary to think in terms of a core platform play. The value lies more in the ecosystem.

A company with an innovative app or a core design competency can be at the centre of an ecosystem, as ARM Holdings is in mobile chip design. In the ARM case, design competency takes the platform's place. ARM organises itself around the task of nurturing the mobile ecosystem of silicon manufacturers, silicon design, and device makers. Haier, by way of contrast, organises around multiple small internal companies, each with an entrepreneurial culture.

- *Data-driven OMs* use data to create decision algorithms to minimise the risk of human decision-making squandering opportunity. In evidence in companies like Google but especially Alibaba, the idea is to generate as much new market sensing data as possible, e.g., via video viewing, blog readers, time spent on product pages and so on, to create signals for change.

  For example, if customers begin viewing more and more videos of electric vehicles, then it makes sense to signal to suppliers that in-car services will increase in demand. But similarly, it indicates internally that some form of business x will be giving way to new business y and that therefore internal change needs should be reviewed immediately.

- ***The Digital Business Operating System (DBOS)*** is an operating model developed by Chinese platforms to integrate their suppliers and physical stores in China tightly. In this model, the data value chain in the Data-Driven OM extends to independent physical stores. Platforms like Alibaba and TenCent sign up retailers to a suite of digital tools as part of their relationship with the platform. In return, the platform provides data on taste trends, logistics optimisation and even the proximity of customers.

- *Flow* is a minimalist framework that outlines new, visual work practices, along with the development of highly visible venues for better social interaction and decision making. Team formation is typically holistic.

  Leadership teams are encouraged to become more peer-like in their decision-making and to coach employees. The framework operates from the principle that older operating models generate a lack of communication and collaboration because of the OM's siloed nature. These silos create an unsustainable cost base and very low flow efficiency.

Flow Lighthouse project design provides companies with small steps, test-and-learn projects that help the enterprise to fix broken transformations and plot a more intuitive route to a new OM.

Consistent with all Flow work, the OM is never a fixed entity or fixed set of rules. OM design has to reflect the context an enterprise finds itself in, and these contexts often change. In that sense, you could argue that Flow is the new generative operating model.

Holding this mirror up to executives gives them the option to act or to plan for a more stable future. They "get" the endpoint of their transformation. It also provides context to the Lighthouse Design.

Developing insights into emerging operating models

As we've said already, you can often see the outline of a new operating model in the transformation work a company is doing. That includes seeing where the fault lines are.

For example, many companies explicitly try to adopt the Spotify model but stop at Spotify's older ways of working (tribes, chapters, etc.). They tend not to realise that what became known as the Spotify Model was merely a way of working at one point in Spotify's development. It is not a model that they would now use.

Advocates though do not take the further step, as Spotify does, of developing an integrated operation. Nor do they invest significantly in the content that supports customers in their effort to bring more success into their lives.

It's also possible, sometimes, to see that the logic of an industry dictates a much more robust use of data. All e-commerce benefits from better data but the trend towards integrating e-commerce with logistics and finance, or integrating more closely with producer platforms, makes data an imperative. However, a company will often be insistent that it must have a full data strategy for the single view of the customer, including a data normalisation project (which vendors are happy to sell). That's a large project, when, in fact, the company could create short term insight through better segmentation. But more importantly, the real purpose of the data should be to maximise efficiencies in the ecosystem. The data strategy is often pointing in the wrong direction.

We suggest reviewing the OM types that we have outlined above as a shortcut to teasing out what an appropriate OM might be.

Please bear in mind, as well, that practices such as offshoring are part of an OM. Very often, offshoring is used as a way to shunt new work to an offshore centre. Offshore firms have also been good at selling their innovation capabilities. That's a big problem. You need innovation and novel applications in house. At the edges of your review, you will see these types of challenges that companies set for themselves - trying to manage teams at a distance, working through subcontractor firms, working on issues that are core to the future. Onshoring tasks can be an essential part of an OM redesign.

The purpose of bringing that emerging model out in the open is to develop coherence. Teams are usually grateful to see what they are creating and modelling!

The analysis, though, has to stem from and reflect corporate strategy. Logical, you might say, but here's the problem with that.

Most corporate strategy documents arrive as huge slide decks (150 slides plus), which is a typical consulting firm output.

Nobody can work effectively off a 150 slide deck. Leadership teams will, in any case, be overwhelmed by daily detail. In interviews and Playback, encourage them to boil their priorities down to the three key things they want to achieve in the next 12 - 24 months. Those priorities will be your starting point for the Lighthouse design.

Be wary at this stage, as leaders do a lot of guesswork around strategy.

The points that might emerge can be things like those below, although you want more evidence than just a simple statement before concluding what type of OM is emerging:

- The company needs to either disintermediate or radically reduce the cost of intermediaries (needs new ecosystem-type model).

- It needs to change to a recurring revenue model (and therefore needs to invest in community).

- It needs to scale an innovation radically (typical of a platform play).

Or conversely

- The company has an explicit dependency on data but does not prioritise it (should think of a data-driven OM).

- It spends too much on maintaining legacy but needs to innovate more (is probably under-utilising Cloud).

- It has a large brick and mortar presence but needs to be doing more digitally (think of the DBOS).

What capabilities do we need to execute against these goals?

What would an excellent execution look like? Are there signs of good performance? How do exemplary companies in the same industry achieve these goals?

Asking these questions can help you to form an impression of the type of operating model changes the company needs to make. Do the answers lead you to any of the models we have written about above?

Visualising the target operating model

There are different ways to visualise a TOM model, and we provide more details on this on **The Transformation Sprint** website. Consistent with what we wrote earlier, we can use the four concentric circles to give quite detailed information in a template format.

Note that open content and APIs are the mechanisms that help ecosystems to grow.

Many of the concepts that we use for OM representation and design evolved out of our work with Flow.

Flow was always an end-to-end framework for understanding how value flows through an enterprise. Our generative operating model is really a way to drag attention away from pure structure (the logistics, finance, technical, distribution elements of a firm) to generative or change-enhancing activities such as value discovery and value management or how people learn.

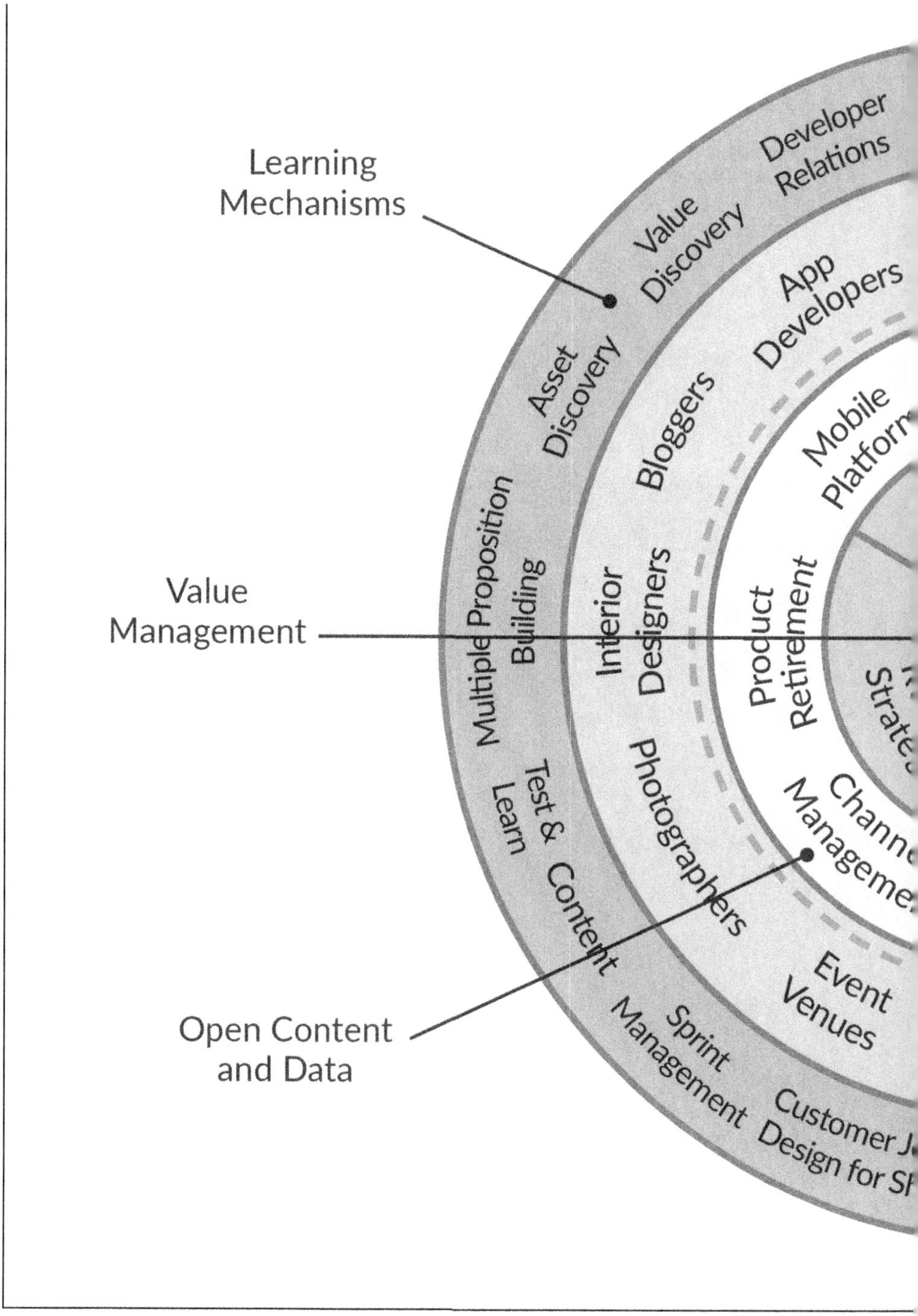

DIAGRAM 7.6. The elements of target operating model

Learning
Mechanisms

Value
Management

Open Content
and Data

Developer
Relations

Value
Discovery

App
Developers

Asset
Discovery

Bloggers

Mobile
Platform

Multiple Proposition
Building

Interior
Designers

Product
Retirement

Strate

Test &
Learn

Photographers

Channe
Manageme

Content

Event
Venues

Sprint
Management

Customer J

Design for S

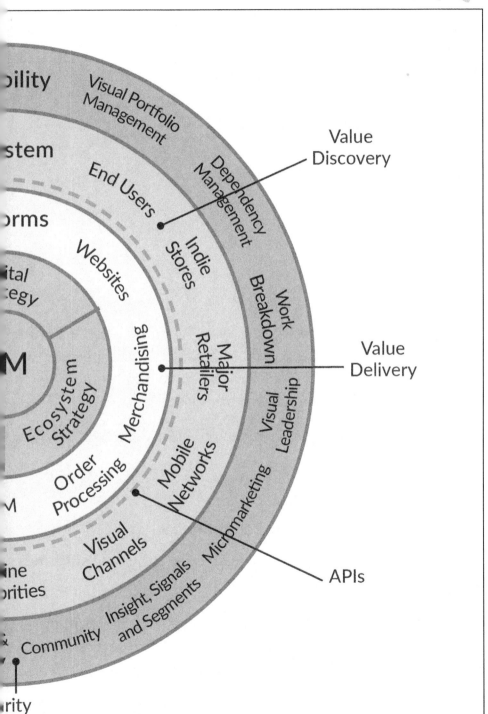

ility

stem

orms

tal
egy

M

M

ne
rities

rity

Visual Portfolio
Management

End Users

Websites

Ecosystem
Strategy

Order
Processing

Merchandising

Visual
Channels

Community

Dependency
Management

Indie
Stores

Major
Retailers

Mobile
Networks

Insight, Signals
and Segments

Work
Breakdown

Visual
Leadership

Micromarketing

Value
Discovery

Value
Delivery

APIs

Playback

Playback arrives at more or less Day 13 or 14 of your Sprint. By this stage, you will have completed all the initial perspective gathering and analysis. You now need to get executives to decide which issues they wish to prioritise.

We will now explain how you run this critical exercise with leaders.

- Artefacts for the workshop.
- Content for your slide deck.
- The type of setting you need and attendees.
- The running order for the meeting to lead to healthy outcomes.
- Ways to support prioritisation.

We want you to come out of this exercise with clear priorities, agreed by the team of senior leaders, such that you have a mandate for the outline solution design (or Lighthouse Project).

Artefacts

We have run these workshops over a whole day, and we have condensed them into three-hour sessions, particularly for online meetings. Increasingly, we tend to favour shorter over more extended ones. It is also easier to design a shorter workshop for remote delivery.

You do not need to complete all the interviews before running the Playback.

The Playback session may also help to identify new interviewees whose insights can feed into the Lighthouse phase. Your basic requirements are:

- The Issues Flashcards (or create them on a Wall inside a visualisation platform like Miro, for remote delivery). See chapter six for an earlier explanation of the Flashcards.

- Strategic Priorities Flashcards (or Miro Wall). We'll explain more later.

- Cool Wall (more on this later).

- AS-IS diagram (use at least size A0).

- Target Operating Model (TOM) diagram (A0).

- Self-adhering sheets to create white walls.

- Markers, whiteboards, Post-Its and an eraser (for a physical workshop).

- The Slide Deck.

Content for the slide deck

Overleaf we have provided a summary of the broad areas of content you should be thinking of.

TABLE 8.1. Content outline for the Playback slides

The agenda for the workshop	Keep it simple and focused. All non-essential information should be limited to the appendices.
The Issues exercise	We use the Issues' Flashcards to create a visualisation of where leaders think the main issues lie. Lead an ice-breaker discussion around these.
The Peep Show: showing the positives and negatives	Create this as two slides, one with short quotes of negative sentiments and the other one with the positive sentiments expressed by staff in a word cloud. Usually the negatives outweigh the positives. Lead a discussion around these.
The Analysis overview	So, leaving aside points of view, what did we find? Start with the overall perspective rather than the AS-IS. What is the market position? How customer-centric is the company? Where does it lag the latest in corporate strategy? For example, we have found companies often do not have a strategy-setting (or adaptation) mechanism. They rely on consultants. We also find executives fixate on their net promoter score or improvements in customer satisfaction surveys, regardless of how weak their overall market position might be. Also draw in some of the main issues from the Issues Wall.
The AS-IS	This is more of a structural statement than a market or competitive statement. You want to show the points at which the operating model is not working, and how this is reflected in the main issues.

A summary of Flow and how it can help: **Value Discovery** **Value Management** **Value Delivery**	We introduce Flow techniques as a different way to think about value creation and processing. We are not trying to sell them on Flow but this gives us an opportunity to reflect back how value creation and value management can work. Consider playing back: Their market segmentation and potential customer success factors. Their resource utilisation (generally we find we can free up 25% of project resources quickly). The complexity of their IT stack, the implications and where they can get quick wins.
The emerging TOM	Here you need to draw out where new ways of work are looking strong (say, agile practices) and where strategy is leading in the right direction, where customer interactions look good, and other sources of strength. Put these in the context of what is making the operating model more modern. Use our templates to show the new capabilities they will need; any legacy retirement that can be achieved; how resources can be liberated and how to grow practical strengths into structural change.
Strategic Priorities	Turn to the Strategic Priorities Wall and reveal your Flashcards. Ask if they would like to add any. Focus discussion on the top three. If you were to do any three things now what would they be?
Potential Lighthouse Projects	You will have prepared three Lighthouse Project options. Present these as potential ways to address the priority strategic issues.

The deck will help you step through the workshop and will also form an important reference point for leaders.

Room setting and attendees

Requirements: The room should be big enough for you to place 10 - 12 Issues Flashcards on a Wall (see below) and 10 - 12 Flashcards for Priorities horizontally on separate Walls. You need wall space too for the Cool Wall and the AS-IS and TOM Diagrams.

You will also need a slide projector and several packs of Post-It notes.

Leave five Post-It notes on the table in front of each participant for the issues exercise. Have five ready for exercise 2 (the priorities).

Transformation Sprints need to have decision-makers in the room. If that's the most senior group, then the majority have to attend.

We have preferred large rooms with plenty of wall space so that we can hang up self-adhesive whiteboards. The white walls will give you plenty of scope to create ad hoc illustrations.

DIAGRAM 8.1. An Issues Wall

We create a Cool Wall on one of these walls. The Cool Wall will have the following headings:

Seriously Uncool, Uncool, Cool, Awesome

You can consult *Flow: A Handbook for Change Makers* for more information.

If you wish to focus attendees on any particular part of the session, you can use hashtags as illustrated in the picture below.

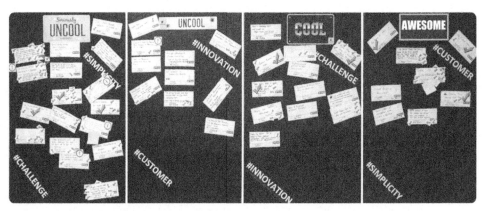

DIAGRAM 8.2. A Cool Wall

The running order for leading the team to healthy outcomes

The Playback should result in priorities and decisions to act on those, even if the best choice you steer them to is a *framework* for action. Executives, and other teams, need reminding of the need to make decisions. There's a strong tendency to treat workshops as if they were away-days.

The order of the workshop should be:

BLOCK 1: Introductions 10 minutes

We prefer introductions that reach beyond the management role and tell us, instead, about a hobby or pastime or belief. In our case, we introduce Fin's running and Haydn's flower photography. We explain why we do these things and their impact on us emotionally. We ask for the same back. You want emotion.

You can hit resistance by asking management to introduce the real person, but it's worth a shot.

We also introduce the exercises and the Walls that we are going to use and we emphasise that it is a day for action and decision making. At this stage, we keep the Priorities Walls and the AS-IS and TOM diagrams covered. But we present the Cool Wall early on. We emphasise that we are going to be on our feet for most of the session, doing things rather than sitting and talking.

The Cool Wall is for people to get up and use whenever they want to log their interest in a point. In meetings people tend to follow the leader so having a place to leave a viewpoint anonymously helps draw out stronger perspectives.

BLOCK 2: **The Strategic Issues Wall 20 - 30 minutes**

Requirement: An Issues Wall made up of 10 - 12 A4 flashcards, as described earlier. Each flashcard should be a short 140 character summary of a major issue impeding the company's progress.

- Introduce the Issues Wall as the main summary of the Playback from employees and indeed leaders.

- Invite participants to join you at the Wall.

- Introduce the Flashcards by reading out loud from the first three to five. If you don't read them aloud, participants will not understand what they are supposed to make of them. Encourage them to come up and read.

- Ask each participant to read through and consider carefully and then place 5 Post-It notes under the issues Flashcards they believe to be most pressing and problematic. They can post more than one per item per card or divide them one Post-It per card.

- They can also make notes on them if they wish, but there is no obligation.

- They do not have to identify themselves on the Post-It, though they can.

Allow fifteen minutes before opening up the discussion. You should see something like this (overleaf).

Note that you have a very visual and speedy way of showing participants what the mood of the room is. It then sets up nicely the next section when you introduce the positives and negatives from your findings.

DIAGRAM 8.3. A representation of an Issues Wall

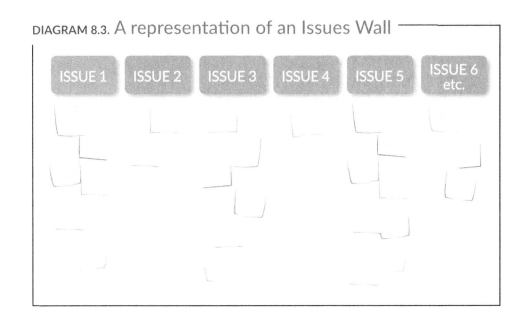

BLOCK 3: The positives and negatives 30 minutes

We create two slides with positive and negative comments from staff displayed as newspaper headlines (or a word cloud). The aim is to present the blunt truth of what employees think of the organisation's challenges.

Sometimes even the positives are seen as negatives! But you are trying to generate debate and passion among people who typically want to be above the fray. Once their emotions are engaged, they cannot avoid the sense that something has to change.

After introducing the staff view, move onto the analysis. You are showing the points at which the operating model is not working, and how this is reflected in the main issues. But always defer to the positives too. In fact, in the TOM section, you will be much more positive. Cover off market position, strategic strengths and weaknesses in the context of market changes, competitor strategies,

the wider context of changing customer needs, and potential trends in strategy that will disrupt this sector.

BLOCK 4: The AS-IS 30 minutes

Transformation Sprints should provide a working diagram of the major operating components of the company, identifying where these work well and where not.

As per the diagrams on page 126, you can place hotspots on the problematic areas of the AS-IS. You need to reference back to the Issues Wall to show the impact these are having.

Almost invariably, executives find it hard to accept these failings when they are in the room together. After all, they are responsible for managing what they see on the slides. However, you can move the discussion away from personal accountability to where it often belongs: the accumulation of structural weaknesses over decades.

BLOCK 5: Flow tools 30 minutes

At some point in the presentation, it is worth introducing the main Flow tools: Value discovery, value management and value delivery. The company will most likely be running a problematic innovation program. There are three variations on this theme:

1 No innovation program with a clear governance structure: new ideas and new work is created on the fly often by the CEO or a senior colleague and is not tied to strategy or a decision-making process.

2 Lean innovation that ends up pushing too many projects into the funnel. Even when some of these

are intended to activate wider changes, their effect is to create large amounts of context switching for development teams. Productivity has gone way down and people are at sea.

3 Too conservative an innovation program, with old fashioned decision gates and larger projects that push value too far into the future.

Value discovery can resolve those problems. Value management can create quick resource wins to divert money to new areas of work such as the Lighthouse. And value delivery can bring some sanity to downstream work design.

BLOCK 6: The emerging target operating model
30 — 45 minutes

You need to introduce your analysis of the type of operating model that is emerging. We have provided summary accounts of these in earlier chapters. The purpose of this exercise is to show that they are making progress towards a better future.

It is tentative and it requires more of their attention. It also requires them to be more mindful of what they are doing. Day-to-day, they are absorbed by troubleshooting tasks and a sense that events are out of control. But you are showing them that logic and order are there, they need to nurture these attributes. The Lighthouse Project is going to help with this.

We also make the point that Flow tools will help but it is not a point to press too hard. A task like creating an Executive Portfolio Wall can be the Lighthouse. It is not exactly what we like to see, but sometimes resources

are badly squandered and the Wall provides a fix to that, helps rationalise workflow and brings a sense of control.

We also like to see companies make decisions about a Future of Business unit. Amazing though it may seem, too many companies rely on their accelerators, hackathons or incubators for their future of business responsibility. But imagining the future is a continuous task that goes hand-in-glove with OM redesign. Very often, executives hear what they want to hear and plan the future as a slight deviation from the present, building on competencies and markets they are strong in or which are just familiar. That's why they don't adapt. We think a Future of Business unit with those two obligations is a worthwhile investment.

BLOCK 7: The Strategic Priorities' Wall 30 minutes

You can reveal this Wall once you feel confident that problematic areas (issues and dysfunction) have been adequately conveyed and understood.

In outline, this is a re-run of the Strategic Issues Wall with priorities for action taking the place of issues.

1 Create flashcards with 10 - 12 strategic options for action. Attach in a horizontal line on the Wall. Familiarise executives with the cards and their content as you did for the Issues Wall.

2 You can leave any number of these blank, but if you do, you now need to go through all the completed flashcards and ask what's missing. We prefer to leave between 2 - 4 blank only.

3 Invite them to place blank Post-Its under those they believe are the top priorities.

4 Discuss those with fewer Post-Its to elicit feedback on the decision-making process.

5 Discuss the main priorities and any thoughts on timescales for action.

BLOCK 8: Lighthouse decision points 30 minutes

Present the options that you've worked on in anticipation of where the team will go. It is always worth keeping one short term fix as part of your armoury. That might be the Executive Portfolio Wall, or a Value Discovery phase. The kind of decisions to push for are:

- How important are short term fixes?

- How does this affect the shape and direction of the Lighthouse?

- A decision to act on the top three priorities.

- An action timescale for the top three priorities.

- Governance for any decisions.

Prioritisation techniques

There are options for how to prioritise:

One is to score the priorities' list according to each item's relevance to the top corporate goals. To flesh this out on a wall:

- List out the company's top four or five goals for this year.

- Provide executives with five Post-It notes.

- Ask them to write their top personal priorities, one on each note.

- Post under the appropriate goal.

Another technique is to score each item according to its complexity and value. Create a 2 x 2 matrix with high value / low complexity; high value / high complexity; low value / low complexity; and low value / high complexity.

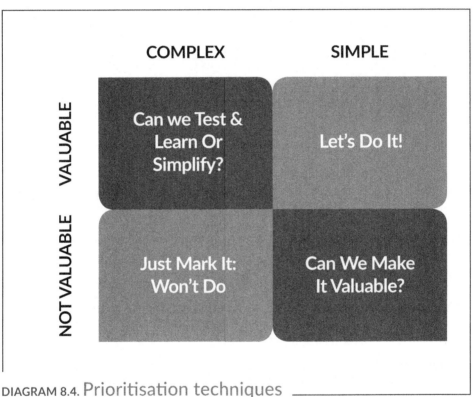

DIAGRAM 8.4. Prioritisation techniques

Score each priority on this 2 x 2. The choice then is to decide actions based on their relative complexity and value.

In practice, both these methods can be used more intuitively. People's gut instinct helps them. It is worth making the criteria explicit even if you do not do this formally. Remind participants that they have to prioritise actions that can bring value quickly.

The Lighthouse

When we first started Transformation Sprints, we used the term *solution design* for what we now call the Lighthouse project. We made the change because it struck us that "solution design" has no predetermined characteristics or shape. You can make up any kind of solution. And indeed you will feel pressure to create one that solves a pet problem for one executive over that of another one.

However, we had quite specific goals in mind for our solutions, so we searched around for a term that did our objectives justice. The solution had to have discipline, and it had to deliver the right things, not play to the exigencies of the day.

In this chapter, therefore, we will explain the principles of the Lighthouse so you can anchor yourself properly in the objectives you are aiming to achieve. You won't be so easily pushed around because you have the charter to outline a project that will help structural change and develop new ways to work.

After we have outlined these principles, we will look at the objectives you should be trying to achieve. Then we will review the design process and give you a working example.

Main principles of a Lighthouse Project

A Lighthouse should be a beacon for longer-term change. It needs designing so that it shows the path from the **AS-IS** to the **new operating model**.

We emphasise yet again that the ideal future state is generative rather than a fixed target.

The project should also create lessons and experiences in how to deliver value at a much faster cadence. And it needs to show innovation value quickly. In short, it has three elements:

- Being capable of solving structural problems in the OM.

- Proving itself as a mechanism for creating new value.

- Embracing new ways to work.

In this chapter, we are not going to do a full Lighthouse Design. That has its own section on **The Transformation Sprint** website. A Transformation Sprint cannot promise a full design because one output from the Sprint is setting up a team to do the project. It is the job and charter of the Lighthouse team to do the full Lighthouse design. They are mandated to take on that responsibility. And it would be inappropriate to hand them a set of instructions. The team has to work in new ways.

For a Transformation Sprint to be successful, you need to arrive at an outline of what the Lighthouse will be. You need to know what it should achieve. You need to give leaders three options for how to get there. And you need their commitment to prioritise one out of the three.

How the objectives interact

The objectives of the Lighthouse outline design (innovating a product or service, doing so in a way that addresses a structural problem, and solving that problem through new ways to work) are tightly bound together.

They all matter because the future state should be one where people are more focused on value and create value through new ways of working.

To achieve this, the Lighthouse scales the company's problems down to one project. If you have a big headache, you take a small aspirin. So likewise, we scale the issues down. We design one project that has those three attributes above. It can solve a problem in an innovative way to show value; it can deal with a structural issue; and it is executed through a new way to work.

Typically, companies that run into trouble with transformations have placed all their hope on the technical side of change. They neglect the business aspects.

When we propose Lighthouses, they can be about content, about distributor relationships or customer journey design. They don't have to be about technology nor can they only be about technology. When the leadership shows the wider team a willingness to sit down and get one aspect right, by investing in the skills and autonomy this takes, a lot more can change.

We scale down so that we can skill up the firm's ability in business agility, once they have had an opportunity to learn what's needed.

The scale-down allows skills' development and quick successes, but then we need to scale back up, and we do that through dividing the first Lighthouse team and

co-locating them with other teams on new projects. We call that cell division and it works brilliantly for scaling multidisciplinary Business/IT teams.

It can be problematic for executive teams to accept this strategy:

- Their status means they want to commission big projects.
- They generally believe they are already doing agile because they've been told so.
- They may have commissioned a consultancy to do a Spotify, SAFe or Platform model.
- The idea of scaling down gives the appearance of change taking a long time, and they want speed.

It is essential to point out that transformation has already created inefficiencies and that projects are running over budget and schedules. Another large project will run into the same problems. Scaling down is the only viable option.

Some further considerations will allow you to broaden the discussion of the benefits of your approach.

- The Lighthouse team should be multidisciplinary or holistic: you can talk to the benefits of team-building and experimentation.
- The team should have decision-making power: you can talk to the importance of autonomy.
- It will create its own charter and define its own ways to work: radical for some companies but a learning experience for senior management to sit back and observe.

- Value delivery has to be on a fast cadence. Project design and work breakdown will prioritise this: you are promising value early on and thereby reducing risk.

- It should address a business-critical challenge: you are taking them on a journey to solve critical issues.

Before we look at the design steps, we'll look first at a few examples.

Three Case studies

In this section we are going to share three case studies. The first two are relatively short, just to ease you into "live" mode. The third is a detailed simulation of a Transformation Sprint so that you get to see the process play out.

Case Study 1: Core platforms and tough choices for everyday efficiency and delivery

Paddy Power, now part of Flutter Entertainment Plc, is one of the most successful online betting companies in the world and provides platform services to other betting companies. It wasn't always so successful. In the earlier part of the 2010 decade, the company's core platform strategy had left it with serious replication problems in its risk and pricing engines. These were absolutely core to the business, as it did millions of dynamic price changes each Saturday afternoon (peak betting time). Rather than one platform, it had seven.

The company ran through the analysis that we have described above and came up with the following options, using an options table like the one opposite:

Option	Platform Strategy	Headwind
1	Do nothing, sweat the assets	Future simplification will not be possible and replacement is inevitable, impacting the business in the future
2	Retire old products to simplify	Can cause conflict with the teams who own the old products (even small amounts of revenue are defended by businesses)
3	Refactor and upgrade current platform	Difficult to get buy-in from business teams unless new functionality is added at the same time
4	Hollow out key functionality and create "super services" with API's into the core platform	End to end changes are slowed down by lowest common denominator (i.e. the old platform)
5	Add a thin layer of customer differentiation onto a Software as a Service (Saas) solution	Can create dependencies on vendors for new functionality
6	Build a new platform product by product	Requires dual operation of old and new platforms during the build and a confident CxO team to give the go ahead

TABLE 9.1. A platform options table

Paddy Power chose option 6, i.e. to retire an old core platform that could no longer scale and slowed down change but was also unreliable.

The team designed a Lighthouse Project to build just one product "end-to-end" to test the theory that a new platform could be built. The time taken for building a new process for one product would also indicate the entire effort to build-out all products, which happened to be two years.

To avoid inefficient hand-offs to any other team, the CTO (Fin) and his business colleagues assembled a cross-functional team with a mandate to be multidisciplinary (i.e., they could do each other's jobs if required).

The team included IT people and business people, but more importantly, it also embraced the technical and non-technical people who were responsible for the old core platform. And this is an essential point because when you say, "Good news, we are building a new platform" what the team that works on the legacy platform hear is, "Bad news, we will be made redundant when the new platform is ready".

In some extreme cases, those people will do their best to withhold information and actively try to sabotage the new platform development. Leaders need to be aware that transformation is not just about product and tech. It's also a transformation journey that impacts careers negatively and positively. People will become your greatest advocates if they have a clear path to follow and a place within the future operating model.

Case Study 2: Core platforms and delivering change for critical business priorities

A leading organisation in financial services wished to become more customer-centric. However, IT, marketing, product owners, and senior management contested what is actually meant by the idea of customer-centricity.

To the marketing department, it was a question of creating omnichannel marketing capabilities so that they could reach and track customers and prospects across Facebook and other social media sites, as well as their own website and mobile.

Like many companies today, they had chosen the SAFe framework to govern the overall transformation process. For the IT department, that meant that any change in the front-end capability (what customers experienced) would take second place to their focus on getting SAFe right. It was more critical for them to learn and master the disciplines of SAFe.

Meanwhile, at a more senior level, the idea of omnichannel excited executives because of the potential for upsell and cross-sell opportunities and increased revenue on the back of a higher average customer spend. They expected revenues to increase significantly by adding channels, even though they were playing catchup with sector leaders and offering precious little that was new.

The company decided to create a new mobile team and a new website team to interact with a services team (who in turn interact with the core platform team). So, four teams, all owning their own mandates!

That is not logical, even on paper, but it is a traditional way to organise. In fact, it meant that there would be no change at the core platform level, and the different groups would almost inevitably be driven by their own, different channel logic. Each of these channels would become one more layer weighing on the core platform problem.

Taking a Transformation Sprint approach, the team could have arrived at different conclusions when looking at the top ten issues:

1 There's little scope for growth in financial service revenues, and omnichannel is at best a defensive posture.

2 Growth in customer engagement in financial services is coming from ancillary services (for example, the provision of data to customers and the support of new commercial platforms).

3 The company has a history of significant project launches that go badly wrong, and its teams were totally consumed with implementing SAFe and hadn't yet managed to get back to their previous productivity levels. Either SAFe was a wrong choice or the timing was working against the overall objectives.

4 Significant numbers of people were losing their way in this new way of working. Morale was low.

5 There was no internal expertise of any long-standing with mobile as a channel or as a technology, because the company had outsourced previous mobile initiatives.

6 The core platform was becoming a liability.

7 The company lacked strong content skills to make use of a good platform and needed to upskill in this area. Having new channels is great but they require new modes of content.

8   Customer-centricity was yet to bake into the culture. Not even marketing understood customer success factors. Market segmentation was very much based around existing products. The company had begun ringing money through the tills, mentally, before figuring out what new benefits they were bringing to customers.

9   Middle management in the business was not skilled at spinning up new value propositions and, as a consequence, became defensive about new ways of interacting with customers.

10 Trying to tie the work of the different teams back to the core platform was going to create dependencies that need strong project management, but as already stated, that was lacking.

The answer to a problem like this is to create a much stronger customer-centricity project. In the case of the Paddy Power project, above, the product range was apparent and very successful. Success was being held back by the core platform problem.

In this case, it is not at all clear what future financial services the customer-base needs. The company's strategy is just to find new ways to sell when, in fact, it needs to find out what new value it can offer.

We see a Lighthouse such as this being staggered into two or three phases but with the customer insight problem taking the lead. It is a standard operating model problem. Companies have jettisoned customer insight in the belief that they can buy the data that will give them a competitive advantage.

But, they can only resolve the core platform problem if they know what the future product range is likely to be.

While the core platform problem is critical to any success, it is going to take months to get agreement on what to do about it. On the other hand the company lacks insight into customer motivation and the skills to use the new channels.

The answer is to set up a multidisciplinary team with a brief to revamp the corporate value proposition around a new generation of products and customer journeys that would take in all available channels. On the back of one of these, it can then choose to refresh the core platform by taking one product and working that through end-to-end, and leverage the SAFe release train assuming that the wider team finishes the SAFe implementation..

Case Study 3: Adapting and redesigning an operating model in energy

Energy distribution involves the purchase and delivery of energy commodities such as gas and electricity through a distribution grid. These were once monopoly businesses. The monopolist both produced (or extracted) and distributed the energy as well as owning the infrastructure for distribution. Change created potentially perilous conditions.

What we want you to learn from this case study is:

1 How different competitive factors affect the design of an operating model and how the OM can provide an advantage over competitors who have inefficient operating models.

2 How multiple factors that absorb vast amounts of time

are symptoms of an underlying structural problem.

3 How a Lighthouse project answers those problems.

4 The balance of scale and resources. Many companies like to create large projects and find small ones irrelevant. We believe the opposite can be true. Large projects absorb resources and push value into the long term, as well as encountering many fail points. Smaller projects allow us to learn and grow.

The background to the main case study

Over recent years, Governments have favoured competitive markets in areas that used to be monopolistic. Energy is one of these, but the same points hold for many markets where there is oligopoly power (banking, telecoms, utilities in general, oil and gas, social media platforms, search, mobile telephony and so on).

There is a well-established pattern in economic development where industries with many smaller players, eventually become oligopolies (where a small number of companies control the market). Fundamental market changes then have a habit of producing new entrants that go on finally to join the small club of dominant players.

So, for the case study, let's accept that a group of incumbents exist alongside multiple smaller companies and also their counterparts from other energy sources and other countries.

An incumbent in gas extraction typically now competes in electricity markets (you will pick up on these issues in your Analysis for which see Chapter 5).

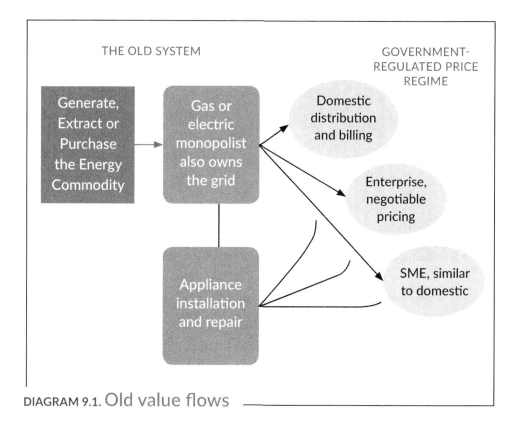

DIAGRAM 9.1. Old value flows

You can see in the next diagram where industries like energy originated.

What's particularly worth noting is that there was no real need, in the days of monopoly, for marketing the commodity (gas or electricity). Given they were the sole source, why bother marketing it?

What we understand today by the mixture of marketing, customer service and billing would, back then, simply be distribution and billing, with an emphasis on credit control. This is, in fact, a genesis story for a lot of today's companies. They grew out of institutions that had no need to excel in how they treat customers.

One could take that argument further and say, marketing developed over the past two decades or more, as a way to generate a sense of need among customers (for fashion, for social advantage, for display) that companies could then fulfil with their own product lines. Those days haven't disappeared but they are challenged by empowered customers.

Let's think about some parallel examples. In refuse collection, or what we now call environmental services, the local authority would have been the monopolist for decades with no need to sell a service.

Even in services like banking, we are generally talking of oligopolistic conditions with a small number of significant banks or transaction processors owning the bulk of the financial flows. In mobile telephony, similar conditions apply. Until the 1980s, these were wholly monopolistic (that means one company owned the whole market).

Monopoly and oligopoly have consequences for operating models, which we will come onto. But they also have implications for how companies think about customers and how they see the role of marketing. The outlook is clouded by a sense that customers are a mass market that can be manipulated. Historically, though, the World Wide Web brought the opportunity to replicate person-to-person relationships, at scale. Too many managers don't think this transition through and bring an old customer attitude to modern markets.

Oligopoly firms therefore tend to run very simple operating models. The incumbent acquires the asset (grid, energy, telephony spectrum) and adds some value by way of its distribution. Over time these models have become more complex.

DIAGRAM 9.2. New value flows

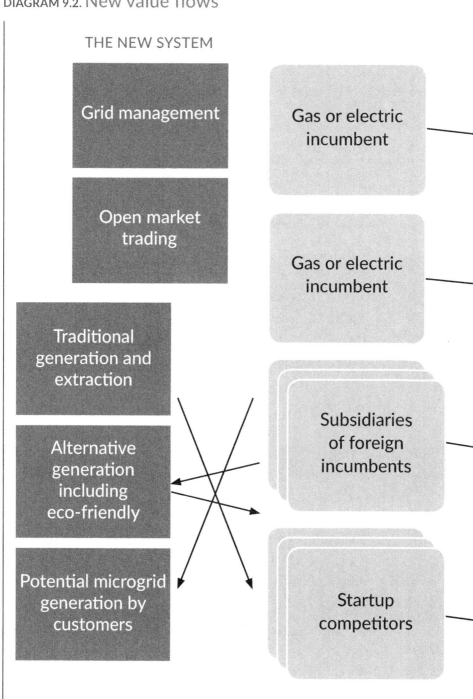

THE NEW SYSTEM

Grid management

Open market trading

Traditional generation and extraction

Alternative generation including eco-friendly

Potential microgrid generation by customers

Gas or electric incumbent

Gas or electric incumbent

Subsidiaries of foreign incumbents

Startup competitors

COMPETITIVE REGULATORY BODY

Regulated pricing

Often forced to follow price setting by competitors

Domestic

Incentivising market share

Enterprise

SME

Promising customer oriented pricing and sourcing

The market has grown away from being a straightforward value chain where monopolies generate or extract energy and then deliver it to customers. There are now more sources of energy, because wind farms, solar and tidal have joined the party. And there is the potential for local micro-generation and microgrids.

The competitive landscape has also seen non-national energy companies enter the market with a mission to win market share, which in turn means they are likely to be price discounters. Their ability to do this depends on their skills at forward purchasing on a variety of contract lengths. That requires sophisticated economic modelling and hence a reliance on data, two facets of operating models that have grown in importance.

There is also scope through smart metering and domestic devices like Google NEST to get more data on consumption and provide advice to customers on potential ways to save money. This offers scope to transform the customer relationship from only billing to value-added services.

Startups have also entered the market and tend to have customer-centricity models, and platforms, that are a street ahead of any incumbent. They might make a promise to maintain a perpetually low price rather than to get involved in discounting and always to source green energy. Their strength is in knowing how to engage customers in the promise of a better future, all around.

While the market has become more complex, however, it is not dauntingly so. It would be misleading to talk of this situation as complex in any deep system-wide sense. It is just a competitive market, but one with more scope for the acquisition of the critical asset; more variable

costs and pricing, more scope for customer-centricity, and more scope for the deployment of intelligence.

The problem for our case study company

The case-study company needs a transformation. And it has focused on:

- Developing a better omnichannel marketing function.

- Becoming more customer-centric (by which it means launching a new loyalty program rather than providing a seamless customer experience whether the client is shopping online from a mobile device, a laptop or in a brick-and-mortar store).

- Deploying more digital processes to reduce costs.

- And being more responsive to initiatives from more nimble competitors. It wants to 'act like a startup!'

The company has to grow new parts of its OM, while at the same time converting other parts to digital systems. It also desperately needs a culture that wants to engage more with customers. It is not fearful of trying out new value propositions but its capability is low.

Underlying all this though, many of its old systems simply don't work well with new ones. It seems to be creating silos rather than integrating digital activity (it has different data teams, a digital team, major projects teams run by people without an IT background, marketing teams that are running mobile programs, and an IT department that is too eager to avoid blame).

These challenges are occurring across industries and across different companies in the same industry. The reason we say that sprints are an answer is simple. When the same issues recur many times over, it is an indication of a structural challenge. The company needs to break through the noise it is creating. And it needs a venue to face up to the underlying problems.

There is a limit to the number of solutions in these situations. We can create templates or matrices of problems and solutions rather than reinvent the wheel each time. That's another critical point. The answer does not lie in a big consultancy report. It lies in facing the facts.

In our case study, the company has hit problems with significant project overruns and failures. It doesn't feel itself to be in a structural crisis, but that is somewhat delusional.

The executive team describe their job as being in firefighting mode. The company is not making critical transitions because leadership is continuously putting out fires. Meantime, the company is wasting resources and allowing inefficiencies to propagate, all shielded by a calm and friendly corporate culture. Sooner or later, the executive team will be found out. An adverse bottom-line event will catch up with them.

You don't have to reinvent the analytical wheel to identify the problems or the solutions though. What we have been saying all the way through this book is that the issues are commonplace. What you need is context.

The variety of predictable problems for the incumbent will come out in your interviews.

The Transformation Sprint process

In this situation, the perspective gathering and analysis should yield an Issues Document (see chapter 6) that looks something like the one we have sketched out below. These are the main problems in our case study example:

- **They have serious core platform problems** because their systems range from forty years old to newly installed. Only the very best CIOs can manage, let alone rationalise, these platforms. They will have substantial technical debt and most likely too many contractors, hired in the belief that technical challenges just need more bodies.

- **They have a significant problem with project failures** that have by now caused severe morale problems. They are continually launching projects that have a specific goal, say a better CRM. But there is an underlying problem with technical incompatibility, age and legacy complexity. They often don't acknowledge this. They focus on the surface problem rather than the fundamental issue. Their projects habitually overrun and overspend, generating a sense of fatalism. People are getting the blame for the overruns, but in reality, their tasks are just plain difficult, especially if you do not acknowledge their origins.

- **Their digital team cannot spin up new propositions.** In effect, it is just a website design and build team, but they lack senior direction to make their web presence effective because as a company, they do not segment the market. Their sense of the customer is not sophisticated enough to build new propositions and to use online channels to communicate with many different types of people with varying needs. They commoditise the market.

- *Customer service is seriously under the cosh*, even with extra investment in call-centre robotics. They lack the ability to plan mixed online-offline customer journeys (i.e. how to promote and sell online the domestic control systems that yield consumption data, and how to integrate this into an engagement system on the web or mobile). There is no clear owner of customer-centricity.

- *Marketing lives in the past* with few ideas for how to front-run the competition. The reactiveness is adequate, but it puts constant pressure on call centres to get their people up to speed with scripts as new offers go live. Without detailed segmentation, there is no way for them to build differentiation other than through branding campaigns. While good to have, these don't bring in new customers.

- *Dependency management is woeful.* The company has a strategy to retire FTEs (sack people) but to function, it takes on large teams of contractors (at three times the rate) under a different budget heading (capital expenditure versus operational expenditure). They hire far more contractors than anticipated. In effect, their internal dependency management, how one team takes work from other groups and advances it, has become over-complex. Nobody understands the workflow well enough to manage it, and the only answer seems to be more bodies. Running staff and contractor teams side-by-side is a cue for massive passive aggression that plays out in more delays and deliberate obstruction.

- *The CEO has begun to micromanage projects* because he is fed up with overruns. Tensions are running high because of his constant presence.

- ***There is no data strategy.*** The data modellers in trading, the most skilled modellers in the enterprise, are distant from what is essentially a data-driven business. Many essential datasets run on spreadsheets, a common problem across industries. But worse, the real data talent is being held at arms' length because it threatens a complacent culture.

- ***The business is doing nothing new***. It has no strategy to make the company different from what it is, an incumbent racing to keep up. There is an almost total absence of vision, mission and goals other than to react faster to price changes. Leadership is embroiled in day-to-day problems and is simply not leading.

- ***Segmentation techniques are very traditional***, emphasising the lifetime value of the customer rather than grappling with what is changing in the customer base or uncovering new market needs. This reinforces the sense that nothing is moving forward.

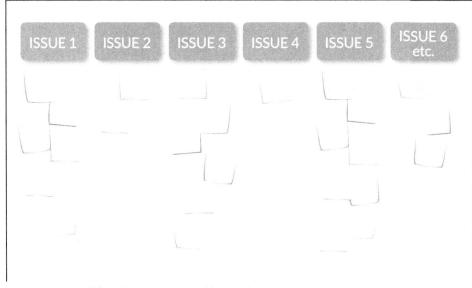

ISSUE 1　ISSUE 2　ISSUE 3　ISSUE 4　ISSUE 5　ISSUE 6 etc.

DIAGRAM 9.3. The Issues Wall again

The leadership team uses the Issues Wall to get a visual sense of where the issues are hurting the most. The beauty of the Issues Wall is that there is no looking around to follow the CEO's lead. Each leader has five Post-Its and creates the visualisation of the team's overall Issue prioritisation log.

In Playback, you can also illustrate how these issues impinge on the AS-IS state. This company exists **between** operating models current and target, building off its traditional distribution model and tacking new systems on to its old core. But it has yet to imagine a model that will work for the future.

Management are stuck chasing their tails as systems and culture cause a continuous stream of problems that need firefighting. And they are all under pressure from a CEO who has lost control. All this gives them less time to think about redesign and remodelling.

You may remember this diagram from earlier. It is one way that we communicate where problems lie:

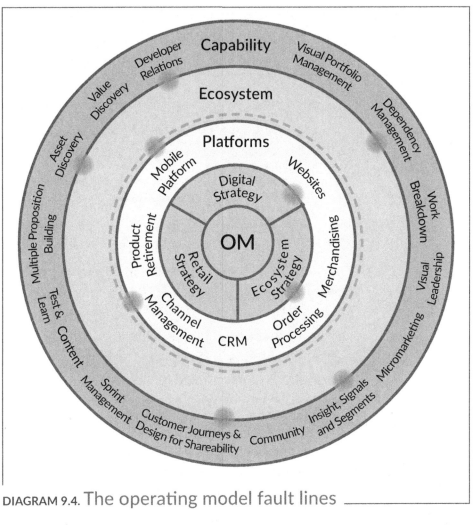

DIAGRAM 9.4. The operating model fault lines

You can emphasise that issues such as leaders firefighting, customer service crises, even the website, are just symptoms. The problem is the OM design.

Remember also that after discussion, you will be asking leaders to use another set of Post-Its to visualise their priorities. The top three priorities might come back as:

1 The need to use data more effectively and with less duplication.

2 How to get closer to customers and increase revenue.

3 The need for a better understanding of resource allocation and how to be more adaptive.

The solution

But how do you go about suggesting a set of solutions using these priorities?

The beauty of offering three prospective Lighthouse Projects is that you can hedge around a little. But now is the time to get up at the whiteboard and begin exploring an outline plan that you can hand over to the Lighthouse team.

1 *There isn't a strong enough commitment to data.* Data projects manifest in different places around the organisation. In the wider world, we are now witnessing the development of data-driven operating models, so here is an important area to explore. As data is often closely related to customer consumption patterns, we may be able to cover off point two with a data OM project.

2 *The customer-centricity issue also stands out.* There are a lot of marketing and customer service issues, but they are symptoms of something more profound. The incumbent's only initiative in this area is to fire up a loyalty scheme, but even that is causing problems. Their segmentation is closely linked to customer lifetime value, which means they are wholly focused on today's best customers, a fault line that we know lulls companies into disruption. Management needs to look to the future.

3 *And finally,* an option is to address the core platform problem head-on. Two main challenges skew resource allocation in many companies. The first is the vast amount of resources that go into managing a legacy IT estate. The second is the extent to which bad projects find their way into the portfolio and create no value. We do an Executive Portfolio analysis to show how these are affecting a company's ability to spend wisely. As well, we use it to show the negative impact on productivity.

We won't address all three of those here but we will add them as case studies to **The Transformation Sprint** website. Let's look instead at how the data issue could play out.

Data as an operating model

In industries where there is a high dependency on commodity throughput - energy, some areas of agriculture, construction materials, waste management, generic food and drinks - data is becoming more important as a mechanism to differentiate services.

For example, in the energy industry, measurement and data are used to model demand profiles and, therefore, to influence energy trading. But data can also be used to support customers to consume less. Consume less? Why would an energy company promote less purchasing? We'll come to that.

In waste management, measurement supports cost controls. Waste pick-up is now routinely weighed and related to a specific account. It means that people on the trucks can't freelance the waste they pick up, and it means users pay on a per kilo basis.

Similarly, though, it can inform account holders of their waste production patterns. That gives the account holder insight to control consumption, that's useful for users and the environment. It is a robust customer-centric ploy. Even though it may seem as though it will cost the waste management company revenues, the reality is that it keeps customers engaged.

Likewise, in energy, smart meters and home control systems allow consumers and businesses to control their bills.

As we transition to electric vehicles and more chargeable devices, providing control will become more significant in the customer relationship. The inevitable increase in demand will make it essential that customers have useful information about how to manage consumption.

Energy companies will see electricity use expand, so their businesses will grow. But as they grow, they can manage the overall change in partnership with the customer. Customers will become prosumers, with their own micro-energy production. Harnessing this in an ecosystem strategy could be very good for business.

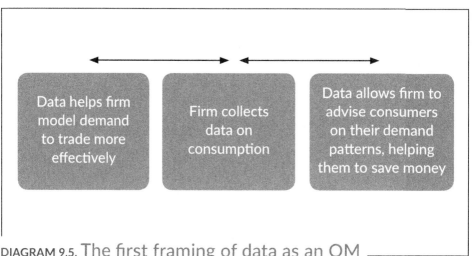

DIAGRAM 9.5. The first framing of data as an OM

A Lighthouse Project in energy would develop a clear understanding of the role that measurement and data are going to play across the enterprise, and that includes trading and customer integration.

For many companies, the future lies in applying a data-driven operating model.

We see that emerging particularly in Chinese companies such as Alibaba. In fresh food, for example, data allows Alibaba to signal the appropriate harvesting time for food, the optimum route management for the logistics carriers bringing food to market and the need for discount offers in shops. They also use data to identify areas of the company where processes are not keeping up with changes in the marketplace.

Overleaf is how that tends to look:

A note on some of those terms: EVs are electric vehicles. Microgrids are local energy grids fed by production from local sources such as solar and heat pumps. In effect, they let consumers sell into the energy distribution network, locally.

A Lighthouse Project for this company would mandate:

- Ways to incorporate data to help manage customer consumption patterns and then integrate this into the trading models.

- Marketing spend and customer engagement strategies (stimulating conservation) in this new, more integrated model.

- Electric vehicle promotion and uptake to simulate and then play out the company's role in replacing carbon-dense forms of fuel.

DIAGRAM 9.6. More thinking on the data-driven OM

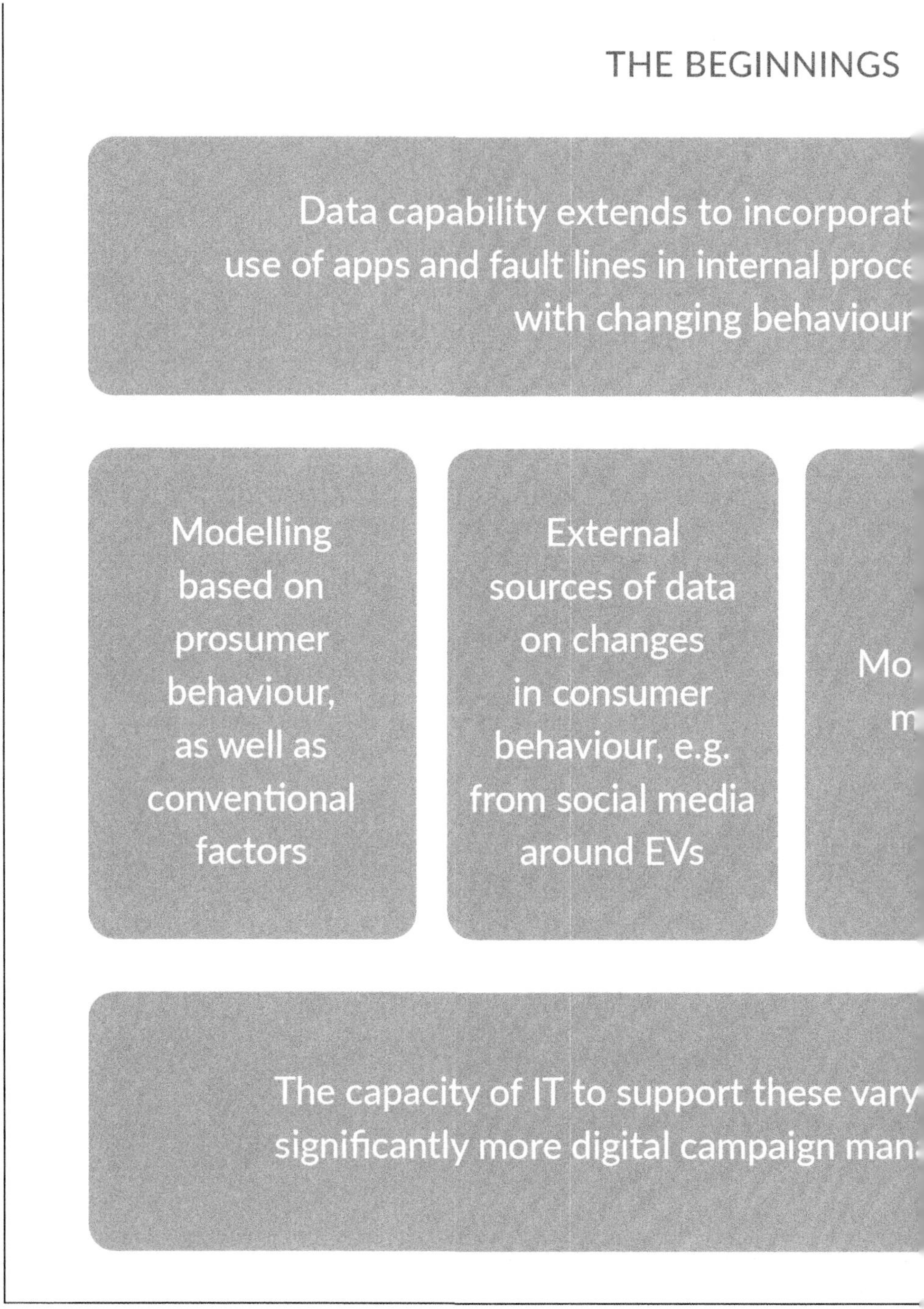

THE BEGINNINGS

Data capability extends to incorporat
use of apps and fault lines in internal proce
with changing behaviour

Modelling based on prosumer behaviour, as well as conventional factors

External sources of data on changes in consumer behaviour, e.g. from social media around EVs

Mo
m

The capacity of IT to support these vary
significantly more digital campaign man

OF A DATA-CENTRIC OM

e consumer data, more micro grid activity,
g. the degree to which marketing is engaging
ed in external data sources

lar
g

Additional customer service and installation capability in microgrids, charging vehicles, charging apps

More robust consumer segmentation profiles e.g. those who buy electric cars and join microgrids

vities such as through apps development,
t, providing insight into customer profiles

- Working with the future prosumer, customers who produce energy.
- Process improvements.

As the thinking develops through an iterative process, it could be that the specific project proposal looks like this:

"A multidisciplinary team will work on a project to map the domestic energy consumption patterns of electric vehicle owners with a view to being first to market with a suite of products supporting affordable electric vehicle use in the context of other domestic energy consumption patterns."

- The first deliverable should be two weeks out and consist of rich customer insight drawn from secondary research, identifying the granular wishes of customers in energy. For example, in an afternoon of research, we found consumers don't know how to assess the quality of electric vehicles, know nothing about their mechanics and maintenance, and need to learn about the panoply of new energy alternatives (for example heat pumps are a total mystery).

- The second will be on the same timescale and will consist of the concept for an electric vehicle club for a sample of customers, along with a content plan for how to develop consumer confidence and be the trusted source of advice.

- The third deliverable at the end of week four will be the initial data set on customer consumption patterns.

- By end month two, we want to see at least prototypes of what the future suite of products will look like and the value propositions we can get behind, with some data validation. Our data modellers should by

now offer insights into future demand patterns and how a front-run with electric vehicles might help our trading position.

It will involve direct contact with EV car owners and the mapping of their energy choices, the pressure on domestic budgets, if any, and the scope for further discretionary spend on apps or monitoring devices. The discoveries should feed into long-range planning in energy demand and prices for the trading team.

Scenarios for enrolling a large segment of the electric vehicle (EV) owner community should examine the marketing and customer service divide and propose new ways for this to be organised.

In effect, we will begin to migrate electric vehicle owners over to a new integrated CRM that will allow us to retire part of our current fragmented estate. We should devise an initial set of data-driven KPIs for judging when those processes will need changing.

As an alternative, the team could decide to work with electric fleet owners.

In designing a Lighthouse around this model, an executive team should be asking for:

- Ideally, a low complexity project with a high-value output but if complexity is unavoidable, then regular delivery. Keeping software development out of the project eases pressure on IT, but by using a holistic team, we can introduce developers to new customers needs and deep market insight.

- Clear statements of the proposed value at each point of the journey. Each deliverable leads with, and how does this contribute to customer success?

- A description of the transition from AS-IS to the future operating model, in outline. That means describing how the Lighthouse will evolve and how it can impact transformation.

- A description of the competitive advantages that will emerge on the journey.

- A holistic team embracing new ways to work.

- A plan to scale the company's core capabilities through cell division.

When the Lighthouse team gets to work on the full design of the project, they should be looking at:

1 Ways to collate external data on EV uptake and new energy opportunities for customers. This should be rapid fire, generating insights within two weeks maximum.

2 The outline of the EV Club concept, with prototype screen designs.

3 Internally generated data that suggests which customers are EV owners and personal contact with a subset.

4 Household budget profiling for the switch from petrol/diesel to electricity and the introduction of micro-generation.

5 The likely downstream value of power management apps.

6 Draft value propositions for this segment of the market.

7 An assessment of how the marketing and customer onboarding functionality would have to change.

For a holistic team, that work should take no more than two weeks. They could be back with a design for prototypes and a draft roadmap within ten working days.

That would meet all the requirements we set out with:

1 Identifying future value.

2 Working at pace.

3 An assessment of an early OM change around marketing, customer segmentation and insight, based on data, with a view to using data to signal the need for process change.

We are also addressing issues such as the absence of an independent Future of Business unit, we are driven by data (and that can lead to a new strategy), we have a small roadmap for revolutionising customer-centricity, and marketing is going to be based on customer success and customer self-help.

By emphasising content over technology, we have provided a way forward. We have also lessened dependency on the core platforms for this project. The Lighthouse team has some tough thinking to do, in planning the future roadmap and cell division.

The Lighthouse design

A draft design is part of the Transformation Sprint deliverables.

1 It needs to reflect the priorities agreed at the Playback.

2 It can address one or more priorities.

3 Identify the priorities and their benefits, describing the high-level value the company gets by solving the problems behind these priorities.

4 Detailed project design should rest with the team.

5 The team needs to incorporate test-and-learn cycles.

It needs to integrate show-and-tell mechanisms in the workflow so that the team is interacting with the organisation (rather than being hived off in the way labs or incubators are).

6 The Lighthouse should avoid chasing down problems in the current state (AS-IS) of the enterprise. There are always going to be problems weighing on executive time, and often these will create performance problems. However, they are often a result of a broken AS-IS state. If the choice is fixing the AS-IS or transforming, the Lighthouse will opt for the project that supports transformation.

7 Design at a high level can wait for a follow-up workshop with executives; if so, then the following questions should be on the agenda:

- What value are we seeking when addressing our key priorities? To fix a problem or change the company?

- Describe this value in terms of specific goals that can guide the team, e.g.

  - increased agility and hence market responsiveness (quantify in revenue terms if possible)

  - potential savings (quantify)

  - staff experience building (reference any HR strategy it contributes to)

  - handover resolution (quantify the benefits)

- Is there a multiplier effect of addressing two or more issues? Describe this.

- How complex are the transformation challenges presented by a Lighthouse project (high/medium/low)?

- What can we do to lower complexity?

- What opportunities exist for increasing value?

- Identify the delivery stages, i.e., when is the value expected, and what is it?

8 Identify the skills needed.

9 Identify key roles and responsibilities.

10 Agree on Lighthouse Governance. Describe how the Lighthouse Project addresses the broader transformation needs of the company and how the leadership team will be involved in regular showcases from the Lighthouse team.

The role of the Lighthouse team

We've seen Lighthouse teams made up of a small number of specialists and we've seen them made up of a broader range of people with varying skills. In one case that meant a data science team along with a developer and a software architect. In another, a holistic team made up of marketing and sales, software developers and a UX designer.

There are some critical points to make about these teams though:

1 They were working outside their day jobs and were not context switching. They had the Lighthouse as their sole responsibility.

2 They were also pioneers, with the full knowledge that they were seeking out a better way to work and a way to solve a structural problem through the project.

3 They were empowered to decide on their ways of working, though they enjoyed plenty of support. In

particular, they learned how to create visualisations of their thinking, processes and solutions. Everything was out in the open so that the collective group could collaborate on every aspect of the work.

4   The charter they create is the charter they work by. For example, if there is a feeling that respect for deadlines is critical to success, they have the power to impose that rule.

5   They were chosen because they have leadership potential. After the Lighthouse, they will go on to lead and seed other teams in new ways of work, usually accompanied by one or more colleagues from the Lighthouse team. That way, they seed new ways of work across the broader organisation through a form of cell division.

6   They were fully informed about the reasons for their selection and this was explicit. They were introduced for their unique characteristics and approach, so everybody knew not only why they were selected but also why their colleagues were.

7   They commit to regular delivery and that means they have to learn how to break work down so that they put value at the forefront of each segment of work design. That's an exciting skill. It means moving away from traditional project work breakdown, to a set of regular milestones that demonstrate clear value to a supervisory group. It involves replacing the question, "how should we chunk this work up?" with "how much value can we see here and what does it look like?"

8   We have found it best when they have their own work environment away from the regular pool. They

need wall space and they need removing from the usual meeting room scheduling so that they are freed up to do good work.

Finally, the leadership team can be fully involved with the Lighthouse through regular showcases. Their role is to remove barriers and blockers, provide expert guidance when needed and, through value management, allocate more people for cell-division scaling. This creates the core capabilities required for their ultimate end state - the Target Operating Model and full transformation.

Final thoughts

Before we go, we wanted to give you a summary of the main points:

1   Transformation Sprints are a way of unlocking the transformational needs of the firm.

2   They help grow OM skills, also ensuring that an OM remains relevant long after a transformation program ends.

3   They can be just as instrumental in helping with the design of a transformation.

To take the third point first, companies tend to aim for a significant transformation using models that might not be relevant to their context.

In the process, these big projects become a source of conflict. They add to existing conflicts that typically grow around dysfunctional operating models and poorly integrated core platforms.

By taking a Transformation Sprint approach, it is possible to accelerate a solution to conflicts and dysfunction. It helps to break through the caution and inertia that big projects create.

To take the second point, we have emphasised that operating models will have to become more generative. This implies that leaders, from the agile coach up to the CEO, become better at remodelling the firm to suit changing contexts.

And to the first point, most transformations become problematic at some stage or other. The worst response to that is to crack the whip and then start micromanaging. That is guaranteed to destroy trust.

DIAGRAM 10.1 Transforming to an agile business

TRANSFORMATION SPRINT	VALUE DISCOVERY	VALUE MANAGEMENT	VALUE DELIVERY
Perspective, Analysis, Issues	Market Analysis	Product Management	Agile Methods (Scrum etc)
AS-IS State and Definition of TO-BE Future Business	Customer Success Factors	Adaptive Project Management Office	DevOps
	Asset Discovery		Continuous Delivery
Leadership Playback	Targeted Innovation	Agile Risk Management	Cloud
Definition of a Lighthouse Project	Ecosystems	Budget On Demand	Test & Learn

THE AGILE BUSINESS

Transformation Sprints are the hallmark of an agile business. It is the entry point towards true business agility and within four weeks, you will begin to see a new way forward.

Equally, you can do regular check-ins with the overall transformation program, or you can use sprints to help you to remodel the OM as necessary.

Operating models frequently change, as we have seen, and the Transformation Sprint is a tool for keeping it relevant to market conditions and ensuring that you have the "bones" to stay adaptive and agile. We recommend doing a new mini-sprint every six months .

Embracing the Transformation Sprint approach will allow you to build those skills across the organisation. Appropriately done, the OM design-skills you develop will help you execute much better on your strategy. It will enlighten and inform you, bringing new value to your business. Before you head off to try the Transformation Sprint yourself, take a look at **The Transformation Sprint** website.

We have compiled all our thinking around the critical changes in the economy and business, on the site. This will help you understand and communicate why your company is vulnerable and what you can do about it.

All these changes and more are impacting your firm. You don't need to do the analysis afresh every time you hit a transformation block though. Use our checklists as your starting point.

The chances are you a connector and communicator, and as such you don't want to be bogged down in analysis. Your role is to communicate effectively. You can do that if you also act quickly. Promising significant change in a short space of time is the most powerful message you can take into your organisation on a Monday morning. Good luck with your Transformation Sprint and don't forget to check out the website at **www.thetransformationsprint.com**.

Meet the authors

Haydn and Fin have been working on transformations for most of their careers. They offer unique insights into transformation not just because of their wide experience. Haydn has a background in R&D, innovation and business applications while Fin is a regular on global top 100 CTO/CIO lists.

Bringing the perspectives of the business and IT together has allowed them to move the debate about business agility and transformation onto a new level. Their most important insights, gained from working with clients around the world, led them to the Transformation Sprint as a way to simplify change and build a stronger learning experience for leaders.

Transformation Sprint builds upon their best selling business books *Flow: A Handbook for Changemakers* and *12 Steps to Flow*.

Fin Goulding

Fin Goulding has earned a global reputation as an experienced IT senior leader improving agile methodologies and implementing extreme delivery techniques within major organisations. A noted bridge builder between an agile IT capability and business strategy, over the past five years he has transformed into a business agility expert. He brings experience as a senior IT Executive in organisations like Visa, RBS, NatWest, HSBC, Aviva and digital startups such as lastminute.com, travelocity.com and paddypower.com together with his Flow Academy practitioner work to advise companies undergoing transformation. As well as being a popular keynote speaker and panellist, Fin co-founded the Flow Academy with Haydn to help bridge the IT-business divide and support leaders and executives in designing successful transformations.

Haydn Shaughnessy

Haydn has a thirty-year background in innovation and transformation. He has pioneered platform and ecosystem thinking, one of the main operating model transitions in the modern age. He has spent decades researching and advising on the impact of new technology on customer requirements and organisational structure and competitiveness. Through this extensive engagement with application innovation, he has been able to lead Flow Academy's work on new value discovery tools and operating model design. A thought leader for several US think tanks, such as nGenera and Gigaom, his work has appeared in the Harvard Business Review, Strategy and Leadership, the Wall St Journal and Forbes. Haydn's work was described by Forbes as "everything you need to know about digital transformation but were afraid to ask."

Printed in Great Britain
by Amazon

21295142R00113